The cost of labor and materials is rising constantly. People are turning to do-it-yourself projects as a means of completing additions and renovations to their houses. If you are a homeowner, a garage significantly increases the value of your property. You will also appreciate the additional stor-

build your own garage manual

age space that your new garage will provide. This book will enable you to make a new garage a reality if you follow the instructions carefully. Should you ever decide to sell your home, a carefully planned and constructed garage will add considerably to your home's resale value.

Build Your Own Garage Manual is a unique guide that concentrates on the process of building rather than designing the garage. Certainly all the elements of design and proper plan detailing are considered, but this is foremost a book that graphically demonstrates the latest in garage construction techniques. Each step of the construction process is illustrated in detail. Several design alternatives are presented for your consideration.

You will understand the construction terminology used in this book as you progress. A Garage Glossary is provided on pages 60 and 61 to explain unfamiliar terms. Study the cutaway drawings and captions shown on page 5 to help you to envision your garage. On pages 63-157 select from a wide range of predesigned garage plans available for ordering at anytime.

Every effort has been made at the time of publication to ensure the accuracy of the information contained herein. However, the reader should check for his or her own assurance and must be responsible for design, selection and use of suppliers, materials and actual construction.

Build Your Own Garage Manual is published by HDA, Inc. 944 Anglum Road, St. Louis, MO 63042. All rights reserved. Reproduction in whole or in part without written permission of the publisher is prohibited. Printed in the U.S.A. © 2004. Artist drawings and photos shown in this publication may vary slightly from the actual working drawings. Some photos are shown in mirror reverse. Please refer to the floor plan for accurate layout.

ISBN-10: 0-934039-46-1
ISBN-13: 978-934039-46-8

Current Printing (last digit) 10 9 8 7 6 5 4 3

TABLE OF CONTENTS

Build Your Own Garage?

The answer is yes! By doing the planning and all or part of the work yourself, you can have the garage you might not otherwise be able to afford. By supplying the labor and buying materials yourself, construction costs can be significantly reduced.

Framing out a garage is not difficult. Standardized materials and construction techniques make it relatively easy if you take the time to plan and work carefully. All the techniques and tips you'll need are in this book. Read it carefully from cover to cover before beginning. It will help you determine the work you can handle alone, and where a little expert help might be needed to do the job right.

You can also learn many construction basics by studying existing garages. Ask your neighbors if you can take a few minutes to review their garages before you begin building your own.

Getting Started

The first step is determining what you want your garage to do. Store your car or cars? Provide a workshop area or additional storage space? If you have two cars, consider a two-and-one-half car design. But before planning too big, remember that your lot must have sufficient space for the garage site and proper setbacks from adjacent properties, sideyards, and driveways. Local building codes often set guidelines in these areas, so check with your local municipality for any restrictions that apply to your situation.

Basic Garage Designs

**1-Car Reverse Gable with
Storage Area and Covered Porch**

3-Car Reverse Gable

2-Car Hip Roof with Storage Area

2-Car Gable

Planning Driveway and Parking Areas

In addition to the structure itself, you'll also want to plan your new driveway, offstreet parking, or turnaround area. The illustrations on this page are designed to give you an idea of the basic space requirements. You may need to alter them to fit your lot, but remember that adequate driveway and parking areas will add greatly to your garage's convenience.

In most cases, short approaches to two-car garages are double-width. For longer driveways, use a single-width driveway that gradually widens to the double-door opening. Drives should be wider at curves because the back wheels make a track with a smaller radius than do the front wheels.

Construction methods for concrete driveways, walks, and parking areas are similar to those covered under slab foundations later in this guide. Local ordinances can apply to these items, so consult with your local building department for specifications covering required concrete thickness, grade and slope preparations, set backs from boundaries, and so on. In general, concrete thickness is 4" to 5". The driveways must be crowned or sloped at 2% to provide drainage. The slope of any uphill grade should not exceed 14%, and any change in a grade should be as gradual as possible.

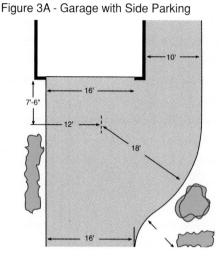

Figure 3A - Garage with Side Parking

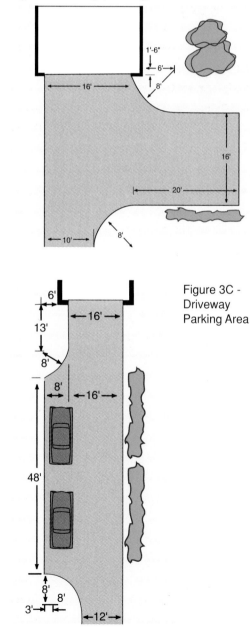

Figure 3B - Garage, Parking, Turnaround

Figure 3C - Driveway Parking Area

2-Car Garage with Loft and Dormers

2 1/2-Car Reverse Gable with Storage

What Size Garage?

You have a lot of options in deciding what kind of garage to build. This book contains designs to help you make that decision, but remember that local zoning and building codes in most municipalities will have some affect on your final choice. There might be lot-size requirements, minimum setback regulations, height restrictions, and certain building materials that must not be used. To save yourself time and future headaches, take a day or so to learn what you cannot do and what you might be required to do. In most localities, for example, at least a building permit will be required. The best place to start is at the local building and zoning code offices.

Take time to consider your possible future needs. Will a two-car garage do, or do you expect that you will need to store two cars and/or possibly a boat someday? Will you use the garage as a workshop? Is storage space in the house running short? Also consider how it will look in its proposed site. Choose a style and size that will complement its environment. Last, but certainly not least, remember your budget. Build for your needs, not your desires.

Figure 4 - Different Garage Types and Sizes

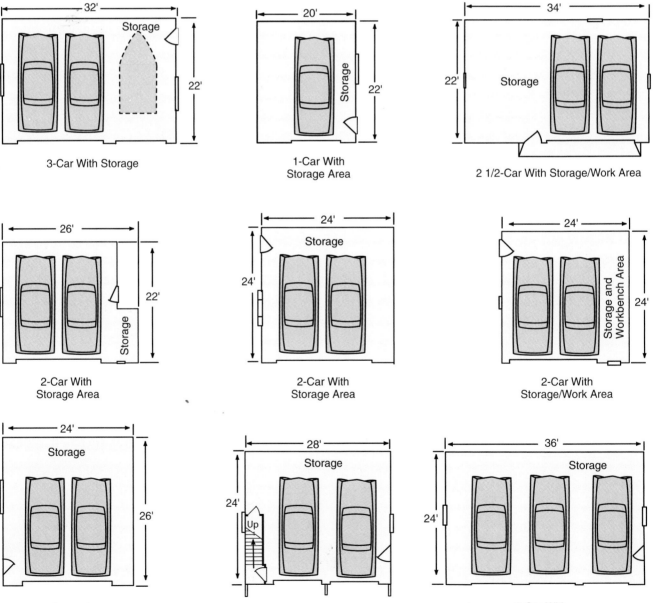

Anatomy of a Garage

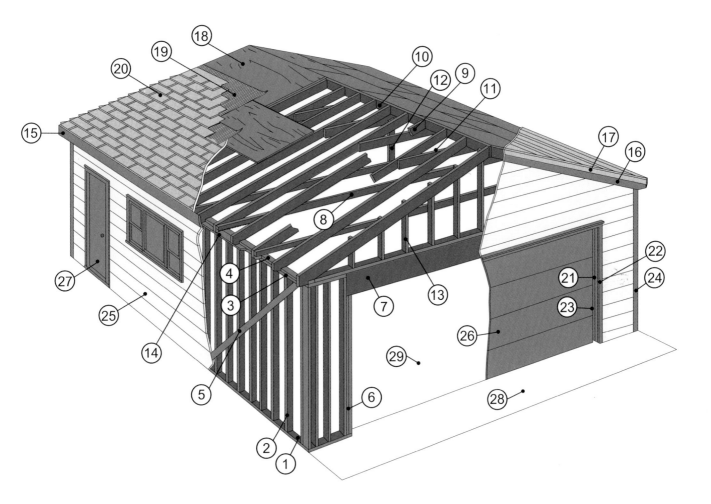

1. Treated Bottom Plate
2. Studs
3. Top Plate
4. Tie Plate
5. Corner Bracing
6. Cripple Studs
7. Garage Door Header
8. Rafter Ties
9. Rafters
10. Ridge Board
11. Collar Ties
12. Hangers
13. Gable Studs
14. Soffit
15. Fascia
16. Fascia (Rake)
17. Gable Shingle Mold
18. Roof Sheathing
19. Roofing Felt
20. Shingles
21. Doorjamb
22. Trim
23. Door Stop
24. Corner Boards
25. Siding
26. Sectional Garage Door
27. Service Door
28. Concrete Apron
29. Concrete Floor Slab

Establishing Lot Boundaries by the Lot Survey

Before you can begin construction of the garage foundation, the precise boundaries of the building site must be verified by means of a lot survey conducted by a professional surveyor. Lots are normally recorded on maps kept on file by the local building or zoning authorities. By studying these maps and records, the lot surveyor will determine and stake out the precise boundaries of your property. By measuring from the proper reference points, the surveyor will establish the front two corners of the lot. These reference points can be the street curb, the center of the road bordering the lot, or special markers placed in the sidewalk. Once the front corners are marked out, a transit level is most often used to establish the two rear corners of the lot.

Once the lot boundaries are set, you can set up lines showing the exact location of the building, taking into account any setback guidelines set by local building codes. The information required to layout the foundation can be found on the garage blueprints. It is also helpful to design a plot plan showing the location and dimensions of the planned garage, driveway, and sidewalks.

Figure 6 - Measuring Lot Boundaries

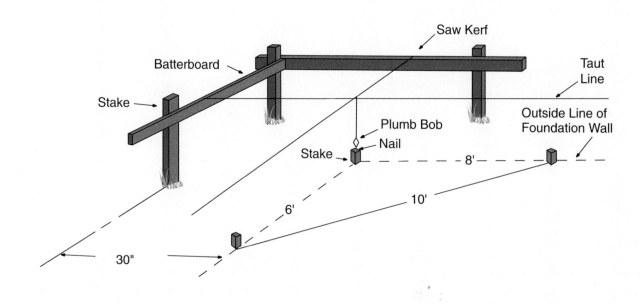

Layout of the Garage Site

Accurately locating the four corners of the building will in turn establish boundaries for the foundation. The site is laid out using batterboards set back from the corners of the planned building in an L-shaped arrangement. Setting them back from the actual building site allows you to maintain an accurate reference point as you dig footings and construct the foundation.

Batterboards are made of pointed stakes connected with 4' lengths of 1x4 lumber. Each batterboard should form an accurate right angle when checked with a framing square. Batterboard tops must be level with each other all the way around. Check for this with a mason's line level.

Layout of the Garage Site

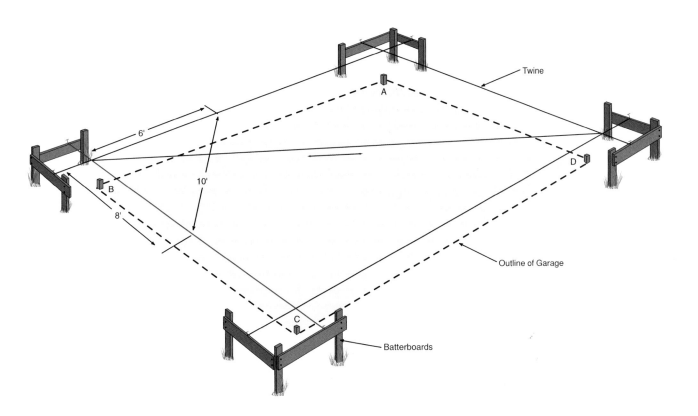

Twine

Outline of Garage

Batterboards

To Set Up Batterboards

1. Accurately locate one corner of the building and drive stake A at that point.

2. Measure out along the long side of the building to the next corner. Drive in stake B at this point. Drive a small nail into the stakes and connect with tightly drawn twine.

3. Measure out the approximate positions of corners C and D and drive stakes at these points. Use a framing square to form an approximate right angle at these corners. Run twine from stakes B to C, C to D, and D to A.

4. You will now erect batterboards and adjust stake locations to form a true square or rectangular layout. Erect batterboards so that each corner stake is lined up directly on the diagonal from the opposite corner as illustrated. Use the line level to check that all batterboards are level with each other.

5. Stretch mason's twine between the batterboards so it is aligned directly over stakes A and B. When perfectly aligned make a saw kerf or cut in the batterboards to make a permanent reference point and tack the twine.

6. Stretch twine over stakes B and C. It must form a perfect right angle with twine A-B. Check for a right angle using the 6/8/10 method. Measure 6' out along twine A-B and 8' along twine B-C. Mark these points with pins. The diagonal between these two pins should measure 10'. Adjust the position of twine B-C until it does and then notch the batterboard at stake C and fasten off line B-C.

7. Using the 6/8/10 method lay out twine C-D and D-A. At each corner carefully measure from the point where the twine lines cross each other to set building dimensions. Drop a plumb line at this intersecting point and set stakes in exact positions.

8. Check the final layout by measuring the diagonals on the layout. They must be equal in length. If they are not, recheck your measurement and make proper adjustments.

Preparing Your Garage Foundation

Inverted T-Shape Forms

The type of foundation you use will depend on your local climate and local building codes. In warmer climates you might only need a simple slab foundation such as those discussed on pages 14 and 15. In colder areas, where the foundation must reach below the frost line, several different designs can be used. The most common is the inverted T-foundation (shown below). Whichever type you require, be certain to build a substantial and level foundation. It can save you plenty of problems later in the construction sequence, such as when you frame and level the walls.

Placing concrete footings and foundations is hard work and can be tricky for the inexperienced. So this is one stage in the construction you might want to rely on professionals or friends with experience in working with concrete. Forms must be strongly constructed of sturdy lumber or use premanufactured forms that can be rented. To keep a large job manageable, divide the areas up into convenient sections that you and your crew can pour and finish in one day's time.

The spread footing of an inverted T-foundation provides good bearing on all soil types. Low T-foundations often have the footing and wall poured at the same time. These monolithic pourings eliminate the cold joint between footer and wall and prevents moisture seepage at this joint.

For high T-foundations, the footer and walls are poured separately. Immediately after the concrete footer has been placed, pieces of 2x4 lumber, called key strips, are often pressed into the concrete. Centered on the footing, these strips form the keyways in the footing as it hardens. These keyway grooves help secure the foundation wall to the footing.

As you can see from the illustrations below, several different methods can be used to tie the bottom or sole plate of the wall framing to the foundation wall. Special ties can be embedded in the wet concrete once it begins to set, but the most common method is anchor bolts.

Figure 8A - Special T-Lock Anchors

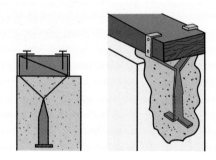

Figure 8B - Foundation Section

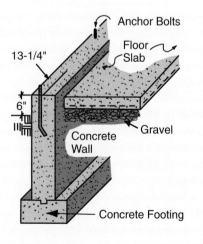

Figure 8C - Slab Foundation Plan

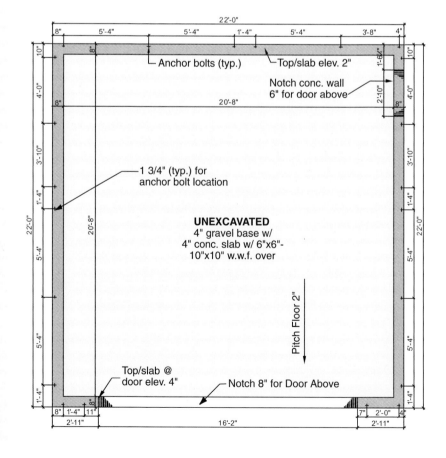

How to Pour a Concrete Footing

Forms for Footings

Typically footings are twice the width of the wall they tie into, but local building codes can vary from this rule of thumb. When the soil is firm and uniform, use an earth form for the footing by simply digging a trench to the required width and depth. When the soil is too soft to hold its form, wood forms for footings and foundation walls will be needed. Several designs are illustrated on the following pages. Concrete is very dense, so build and reinforce the forms strongly. Remember, if you plan to construct a masonry wall on the footing, its top surface must be as level as possible. See page 16 for estimating materials and concrete amounts.

1. **Lay out** the footings using twine and batterboards as a guide for the trench. Use twine as a guide for your forms once the trench is dug.

2. **Level** the bottom of the trench and tap it firm. On sloping ground, use a stepped trench. The trench bottom must be below the frost line.

3. **Build** the forms using the batterboards as a guide for positioning. Support reinforcing steel using brick or stone. Suspend the keyway strip from cleats as shown.

4. **Coat** the forms lightly with release agent. Pour the concrete into the forms, working out air pockets with a flat shovel. Work the concrete into all corners and along edges of the form.

5. **Level** the concrete with the top of the form using a straight length of short lumber as a screed. Work back and forth in a short sawing motion. Knock down high spots and fill all voids. Remove the keyway strip as soon as the concrete will hold its shape.

6. **Cover** it with burlap or plastic sheeting to retain moisture, and lightly spray the concrete with water once or twice daily to keep the surface wet during curing. In hot weather climates cure the concrete for four days.

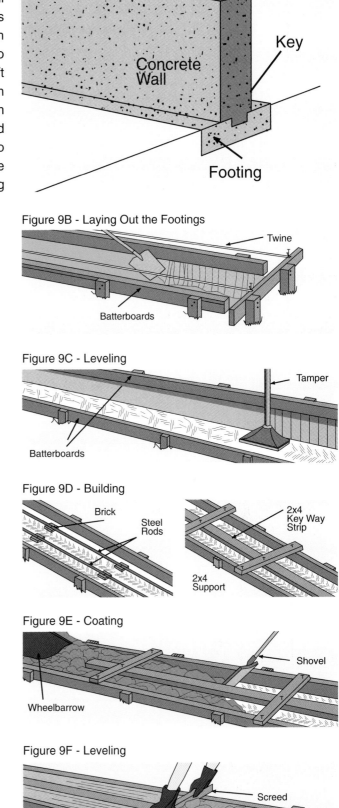

Figure 9A - Footing Cross Section

Key

Concrete Wall

Footing

Figure 9B - Laying Out the Footings

Twine

Batterboards

Figure 9C - Leveling

Tamper

Batterboards

Figure 9D - Building

Brick

Steel Rods

2x4 Key Way Strip

2x4 Support

Figure 9E - Coating

Shovel

Wheelbarrow

Figure 9F - Leveling

Screed

Formwork for Foundation Walls

Once you understand the principles of formwork for concrete walls, you should be able to handle the framework for your garage's foundation wall. Most importantly, the form must be strong enough to withstand the pressure of the wet concrete and the rough treatment it will receive during the pour.

Foundation wall forms are constructed of plywood sheathing, 2x4 lumber framing and studs, wooden spacers, and wire ties. Sheathing forms the mold. The frame and studs support the sheathing. Spacers maintain wall thickness, support the form, and resist pressure exerted by the concrete. Ties hold the form sides together (see Figure 10A).

You may want to explore the option of renting concrete forms, if available in your area. This may save you time and labor preparing wood forms. Wall lengths and heights should be considered when determining which choice you make.

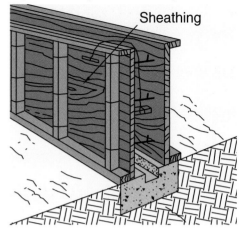

Figure 10A - Plywood Sheathing

Sheathing

Building Forms

Build long forms in sections. The individual sections should be slightly taller than the planned finished foundation wall and no more than 8' in length.

With the lumber laying flat on the ground, construct a frame of 2x4s on edge. Next, nail 2x4 studs into this frame, spacing studs on 16" centers, closer if the wall is particularly thick and will be poured all at one time.

The studded frame is now ready for the sheathing, either 1/2" or 5/8" thick plywood. Lay the sections down, sheathing sides face to face so you can drill holes for the wire ties. Drill 1/8" holes for the wire ties adjacent to the studs as shown. Plan on using plenty of ties to hold the forms together.

Spacers and ties are used to assemble the sections and maintain the proper spacing between them. Spacers are made of 1x2 or 2x4 lumber cut to the same length as the finished wall thickness. Plan to put in spacers every 2' both vertically and horizontally. Wire ties should be made of heavy gauge (8 or 9 gauge) iron wire. Cut the ties long enough to encircle opposing studs on either side of the forms, plus enough excess to comfortably twist the ends together.

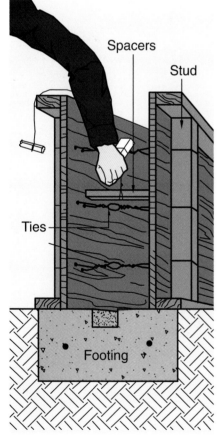

Figure 10B - Using Spacers and Ties

Spacers

Stud

Ties

Footing

Tilt the two sections upright, face to face, and spaced at the wall thickness. Tack the sections together with several crosspieces to make working easier. Thread the 8 to 9 gauge wire ties through the form and around the studs, twisting the wire ends together. Place a 1x2 or 2x4 spacer near the tie.

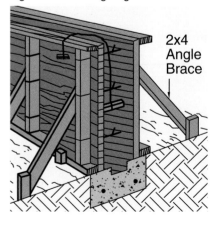

Figure 10C - Using Angle Braces

2x4
Angle
Brace

Place a stick between the wires inside the form and twist the wire tight as illustrated. Do this for all spacers and ties. Tie pull wires on all spacers you will not be able to reach when the pour begins. You must remove all spacers as the pour proceeds (see Figure 10B).

Formwork for the Foundation Walls

Place the assembled form in position on the footer. Assemble additional sections, butting sections together and nailing through adjacent framing members to create the finished continuous wall form. The running length of the forms should be slightly longer than the planned wall length so that you can cleat in stop boards at the end of the forms.

A properly constructed form is self-supporting, but it must be plumbed and tied in place with braces so it will stay in position during the pour. Nail the bottom of the form to stakes driven firmly in the ground. This will prevent lifting. Prevent lateral movement by installing 2x4 angle braces (see Figure 10C).

Prior to making the pour, coat the forms with concrete release agent to make it easier to remove the form. See page 16 for the tools you'll need to place the concrete, plus tips on estimating the amount of concrete needed.

Casting a Concrete Wall

Once the foundation footing has been placed and properly cured, you can set the wall forms in place, align, plumb, and secure them, and then make the wall pour. The steps involved in this process include: mounting the forms, pouring and tamping the concrete, striking, floating, and troweling the top edge smooth to accept the bottom plate, and installing the anchor bolts or special anchor ties.

1. Mount the forms on the cured footing, centering them over the keyway. See page 10 for more details on securing the forms in place. Snap chalk lines along the inside of the forms to show the desired height of the foundation wall if level with the top of the form.

Figure 11A - Mounting

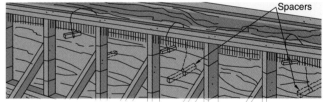

2. Pour the concrete into the forms, working in 6- to 8-inch layers. Do not stop the work once you begin, or "cold joints" between layers will result and cause cracks in the foundation wall. Work the concrete well up against the sides of the form. Tapping the side of the forms with a hammer will help settle the concrete and avoid air pockets. Pull out the spacers as you proceed.

Figure 11B - Pouring

3. Strike the concrete level with the top of the form or your chalk line using a board as a screed as you did with the footing. For a smoother surface, work the top surface with a wooden or steel trowel.

Figure 11C - Striking

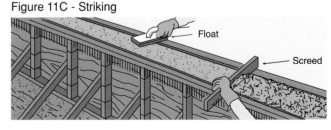

4. Insert the anchor bolts at the proper spacing as soon as the concrete is firm enough to support them if you are going to use anchor bolts or anchor ties to secure the framing sill to the foundation. Cure the concrete for four days as you did the footing. Remove the forms after curing.

Figure 11D - Inserting Anchor Bolts

Building Concrete Block Foundation Walls

Concrete block can also be used to construct the foundation wall on the footing. The running bond shown in these illustrations is most commonly used. It allows the block cores to line up, making steel reinforcing and grouting easy.

Use the same type of mortar that is used in bricklaying, but mix it a little on the stiff side to make buttering the block a little easier. The mortar will also be less likely to squeeze out of the joints. Also do not wet the block before beginning work as you would do with brick.

In regions where hurricane and high winds are a factor special reinforcing may be required. Check with your local building official or building department.

1. Start the lead in a corner, laying a bed of mortar 2" thick for three or four blocks. Lay the corner block carefully and press it down to an accurate 3/8" thick mortar joint. Butter the ends of the next blocks and place each 3/8" from the previous block. Use a level to align, level, and plumb the lead.

2. Continue laying block to complete the lead. Check for squareness at the corner. Use a mason's line to maintain a straight line as you work. All mortar joints are 3/8" wide.

3. Begin leads at each corner and work to the middle. Lay blocks between the leads. To fit the closure block, spread mortar on all edges of the opening and butter the ends of the closure block. Set it carefully in place and check alignment, levelness, and plumbness.

4. With one course remaining, cover the cores with metal screening, this will be used to cap the wall. Fill the cores in the top course with mortar.

5. You can now sink anchor bolts or ties into the mortar filled top course. This will tie down the sill plate on which the garage framing will rest.

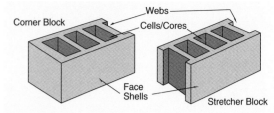

Figure 12A - Concrete Blocks

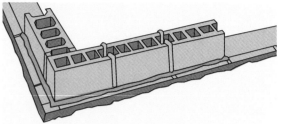

Figure 12B - Starting the Lead

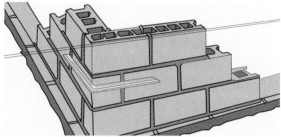

Figure 12C - Laying Blocks Using Mason's Line

Figure 12D - Fitting Closure Block

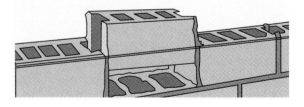

Figure 12E - Fill Cores with Mortar

Figure 12F - Add Anchor Bolts and Bottom Plate

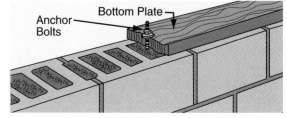

Pouring a T-shaped Foundation Concrete Floor

Placing a concrete floor inside a T-foundation is similar to placing a slab foundation as described on pages 14 and 15. Rather than using forms, the foundation walls are the outside boundaries of the floor. Be sure the area inside the foundation boundaries is properly backfilled, leveled, and prepared with a gravel base and reinforcing mesh set on stones to raise it slightly off the gravel.

Pouring a large slab is hard work so be sure you have two or three helpers, one or two wheelbarrows and shovels, plus all the concrete finishing tools you'll need (see page 16).

The height of the foundation walls makes screeding over the entire length of the slab impossible, so stake a number of temporary screeding guides inside the foundation. These will help you level the concrete to the correct thickness, usually 4". Once the initial screeding is complete, the guides are pulled out and these voids filled with concrete. You can also use a wide wooden darby to level the concrete.

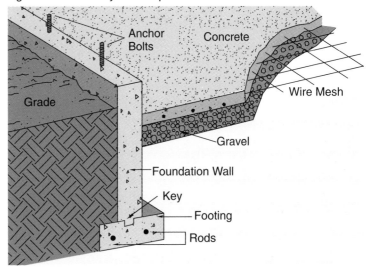

Figure 13A - Anatomy of T-shaped Foundation with Concrete Slab Floor

As the work progresses, watch the concrete carefully. In hot or windy weather, the first sections might be setting up too fast while you are still pouring the remaining sections. If this is the case, some members of your crew will have to begin finishing work a little sooner than planned. Never add water to the concrete to keep it workable until you are ready to finish the concrete.

After each section has been screeded, use a wooden bull float or darby to smooth it. Once the initial smoothing has been completed, wait for the concrete to lose its initial shine before beginning final troweling. For a smooth finish use a wooden float. A really slick finish requires a steel trowel. For large slabs, use a rented power trowel.

Figure 13B - Bull floating levels ridges and fills voids left after striking. It is used for large areas.

Bull Float

Foundation Details for Turned Monolithic Slabs

If you live in an area where frost upheaval is not a problem, a basic slab foundation can be used for your garage. Again, check the local building requirements in your area, and follow their specifications. Here's a checklist of common code requirements:

❏ Slab thickness of 4" with the top of the slab set a minimum of 6" above the surrounding soil.

❏ A footing ditch dug around the perimeter of the slab – 6" wide at the base of the trench and 12" deep or deeper, depending on frost or grade conditions. Footing must contain a layer of reinforcing steel rod 3" up from the base of the footing trench.

❏ You'll need a gravel base under the slab 3" to 4" thick. A layer of 6" square welded wire mesh must be placed in the slab. Raise this wire mesh 2" off the gravel using stones, brick halves, or broken concrete to support it.

❏ Anchor bolts or ties embedded in the footing to accept the mudsill for framing the garage. Use 10" long anchors embedded 7" deep in concrete no more than 6' on centers and not more than 12" away from each end with a minimum of 2 anchors per mudsill. Do not place anchors in doorways.

Figure 14A - Slab Foundation Plan

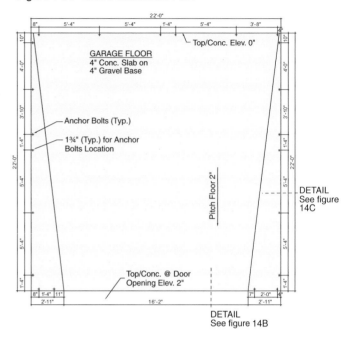

Figure 14B - Apron Formwork

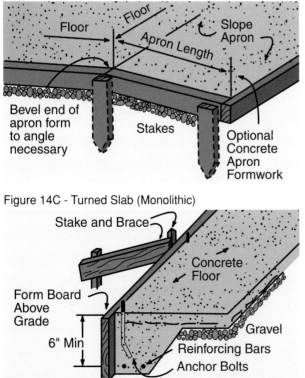

Figure 14C - Turned Slab (Monolithic)

Slab Forms

Level the site. Small depressions can be filled with gravel and concrete. Use 2x8 lumber for the forms and brace it securely. Begin laying out the forms at the highest point of the site and work to the lowest. The top of the forms should be perfectly level. In some cases, you might prefer a slope of 1/4" per 1'-0" toward the overhead garage door location to help with drainage. Double-check dimensions and squareness by measuring the diagonals across the forms. Once forms are square and level, install bracing stakes every 3' or so on the outside face of the forms. Be sure to use sufficient bracing driven well into firm ground. The inside dimensions of the forms will be the finished outside dimension of the slab, exclusive of any apron.

This apron can be poured as part of the slab or added later. If it is part of the slab, bevel apron form boards so the apron slopes to a point level or slightly above the driveway surface.

Once the forms are in place, dig the required footing trench at the inside form perimeters and place the required reinforcing steel in the trench. Lay the gravel base and wire mesh according to code requirements, and wet the gravel before the pour (See page 16 for tools needed and estimating concrete needs).

Pouring the Concrete Slab

Have the local building inspector check the forms prior to the pour date. If electrical service is desired, place the electrical conduct in proper location prior to the pour.

Placing

Have adequate help, wheelbarrows, and tools ready when the concrete truck arrives. Start by pouring in the area farthest away from the truck, using wheelbarrows to move the concrete. Begin by filling the footing trench. For larger areas, break the work into smaller sections by installing temporary screeding guides. When one section is poured move to the next section while helpers screed off the first (Figure 15B). Rap on the outside of the form boards to help settle the concrete. Be sure all voids are filled. Pay special attention along the perimeters of the form boards. Remove the temporary screed guides while filling in these voids.

Finishing

Once the concrete has lost its initial shine, begin finishing it with a bull float. Larger floats have a handle like a broom. If you are using smaller hand floats, use toe and knee boards placed on the concrete so you can kneel on the concrete without leaving much of an impression. Move the float in long sweeping motions (Figure 15C).

Anchor bolts should be placed after the concrete has been screeded and bull floated. Place the bolts 1-3/4" away from the edge of the slab. Double-check spacing of bolts and alignment (Figure 15D).

For a coarser finish, bull floating is all that is required. For a slicker, smoother finish, use a steel trowel to go over the work once bull floating is complete. Use a light touch so you don't gouge the concrete surface. Before the concrete hardens completely, take a trowel and cut between the edge of the concrete and the form.

Curing

Once all finishing is completed, mist down the slab with water, and cover it with a layer of plastic or burlap. Keep the surface moist for four days as the concrete cures.

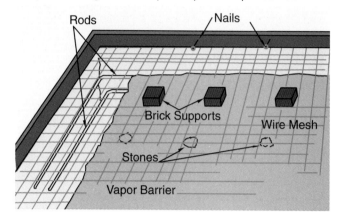

Figure 15A - Steel reinforcing rods and wire mesh are laid into place over gravel and optional plastic vapor barrier.

Rods · Nails · Brick Supports · Wire Mesh · Stones · Vapor Barrier

Figure 15B - Workers level concrete slab with a strike board.

Figure 15C - Smooth concrete surface with a bull float.

Figure 15D - Add anchor bolts.

Some of the Tools Needed

Tamber

Wheelbarrow

Mason's Trowel

Hammer

Kneeler and Pads

Hand Sledge

Striker

Bull Float

Shovel

Broom

Mason's Level

Hand Darby

Carpenter's Square

Edger

Steel Trowel

Groover

Wood Float

Chalk Line

Tape Measure

Twine

Calculating Concrete Volume

Concrete is measured in cubic yards. To calculate cubic yards, multiply thickness (in inches) x width (in feet) x length (in feet) and divide by 12. This gives cubic feet. Divide this number by 27 to determine cubic yards. Take measurements carefully. While you do not want to order more than your needs, being short can cause major problems.

Estimating Cubic Yards of Concrete

		Thickness (inches)	
		4	5
Area in sq. ft. (width x length)	10	0.12	0.15
	25	0.31	0.39
	50	0.62	0.77
	100	1.23	1.54
	200	2.47	3.09
	300	3.70	4.63

For Slab[*]

To find the amount of concrete required for a 4" thick driveway 20 ft. wide by 20 ft. long, for example, first figure the number of square feet by multiplying:

20 ft. x 20 ft. = 400 sq. ft.

Then add the appropriate amounts from the table:

300 sq. ft. = 3.70 cu. yd.
+100 sq. ft. = 1.23 cu. yd.
400 sq. ft. = 4.93 cu. yd.

With a perfect subgrade and no losses from spillage, 5 cu. yd. might be enough. But for insurance against contingencies, the order should be increased to 5-1/2 cu. yd. It is always better to have some concrete left over than run short.

[*]Does not allow for losses due to uneven subgrade, spillage, etc. Add 5-10 percent for such contingencies. Does not allow for turn-down areas.

Choosing Lumber for Framing

Nearly all types of general construction are done using softwoods, such as Douglas fir or southern pine. As a rule softwoods are less expensive, easier to work with, and more readily available than hardwoods, which are normally reserved for fine finishing work.

Lumber Sizes

In general, construction softwood lengths run from 8' to 22' in 2' increments. *Dimension lumber*, graded primarily for strength, is used in structural framing. These pieces range from 2" to 4" thick and are at least 2" wide. *Beams* and *stringers* are structural lumber 5" thick or more, having a width at least 2" greater than the thickness. *Posts* and *timbers* are heavy construction members 5" x 5" or larger with a width not exceeding thickness by more than 2".

The actual final dimensions of lumber are slightly smaller than the nominal dimensions. The chart to the right lists nominal and actual width and thickness for common structural lumber.

Estimate a list of materials from your plans, listing the quantity, size, and length of the pieces you'll need. Prices will be by the linear foot or by the board foot for larger orders. Linear feet considers only the length of the piece, for example, 20 2x4s, 10' long or 200 linear feet of 2x4. However, board feet pricing considers total volume, for example, a 2x4 that is 10' long would be (2 x 4 x 10) divided by 12 = 6.66 or 6-2/3 board feet.

Select lumber that is seasoned or dried. Green lumber can cause problems as it shrinks. Dimension lumber is usually stamped **MC-15** (15% moisture content) or **S-DRY** (19% moisture content or less).

When you can, select vertical grain lumber and be on the lookout for the common lumber defects shown in Figure 17A.

Engineered Lumber

Due to recent developments in timber cutting practices and the reduced availability of certain sizes of framing lumber, engineered lumber manufactured from plywood, wood chips, and special glue resins offers an attractive alternative to dimensional lumber used for joists, beams, headers, and rafters. Unlike sawn dimensional lumber, engineered lumber is a manufactured product that will not warp and shrink over time.

Engineered lumber is manufactured to meet stringent criteria for strength, uniformity, and reliability. Glu-lam beams offer great strength over spans. Wood I-beams provide a lightweight alternative to conventional joists or rafters. Some typical laminated veneer lumber products are shown to the right.

Standard Dimensions of Surfaced Lumber

Nominal Size	Surfaced (Actual) Size
1 x 2	3/4" x 1-1/2"
1 x 3	3/4" x 2-1/2"
1 x 4	3/4" x 3-1/2"
1 x 6	3/4" x 5-1/2"
1 x 8	3/4" x 7-1/4"
1 x 10	3/4" x 9-1/4"
1 x 12	3/4" x 11-1/4"
2 x 3	1-1/2" x 2-1/2"
2 x 4	1-1/2" x 3-1/2"
2 x 6	1-1/2" x 5-1/2"
2 x 8	1-1/2" x 7-1/4"
2 x 10	1-1/2" x 9-1/4"
2 x 12	1-1/2" x 11-1/4"
4 x 4	3-1/2" x 3-1/2"
4 x 10	3-1/2" x 9-1/4"
6 x 8	5-1/2" x 7-1/2"

Figure 17A - Lumber Defects

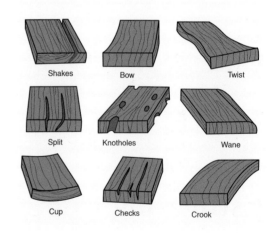

Figure 17B - Engineered Lumber

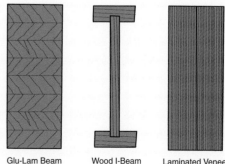

Glu-Lam Beam   Wood I-Beam   Laminated Veneer (Micro) Beam

Nails and Fasteners for Framing and Finishing

Nails are the most common fastener used in framing and construction. Nail lengths are indicated by the term **penny**, noted by a small letter d. In most cases, nails increase in diameter as they increase in length. Most framing for heavier construction is done with common nails. The extra thick shank of common nails has greater strength than most other types. A wide thick head spreads the load and resists pull-through. The larger head also makes a good target for a hammer.

Box nails are similar in shape and use to common nails, but they have a slimmer shank that is less likely to split wood. Finishing nails are used in work where you do not want the nail head to show such as in trim and fascia work. Casing nails, similar to finishing nails but with a thicker shank and angular head, are used for heavier work such as adding casings around windows and doors.

Spiraled shanks rotate slightly for better holding power as you drive the nail in wood. Annular-ring nails also provide extra holding power, especially in softer woods.

Discuss your project with your local hardware or building supply dealer to determine the best nail and fastener selections for the project.

Screws create neat, strong joints for finished work, such as door and window treatments. Heavy-duty lag screws are also used in some types of heavier framing and construction.

Figure 18 - Different Types of Fasteners

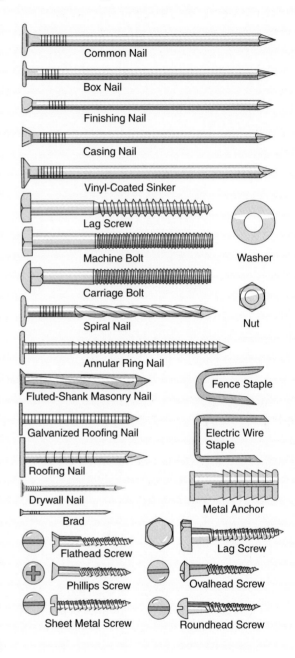

Table of Common Nails

Size	Length	Gauge	# per lb.
2d	1"	15	840
3d	1 1/4"	14	540
4d	1 1/2"	12 1/2	290
5d	1 3/4"	12 1/2	250
6d	2"	11 1/2	160
7d	2 1/4"	11 1/2	150
8d	2 1/2"	10 1/4	100
9d	2 3/4"	10 1/4	90
10d	3"	9	65
12d	3 1/4"	9	60
16d	3 1/2"	8	45
20d	4"	6	30
30d	4 1/2"	5	20
40d	5"	4	16
50d	5 1/2"	3	12
60d	6"	2	10

Finishing Nail Selection Chart

Size	Length	Gauge	# per lb.
2d	1"	16	1000
3d	1 1/4"	15 1/2	870
4d	1 1/4"	15	600
6d	2"	13	310
8d	2 1/2"	12 1/2	190
10d	3"	11 1/2	120

Screw Selection Chart

Size	Length	Gauge	# per lb.
0	1/4-3/8	9	1/2-3
1	1/4-1/2	10	1/2-3 1/2
2	1/4-3/4	11	5/8-3 1/2
3	1/4-1	12	5/8-4
4	1/4-1 1/2	14	3/4-5
5	3/8-1 1/2	16	1-5
6	3/8-2 1/2	18	1 1/4-5
7	3/8-2 1/2	20	1 1/2-5
8	3/8-3	24	3-5

These tables show the approximate number of nails you get in a pound. You'll need more pounds of larger sizes to do a job. For outside jobs, get galvanized or cadmium-plated nails. Aluminum nails are a bit expensive unless you are doing a smaller project.

This chart shows sizes and the lengths in which they're available. The larger sizes come in longer lengths. Most jobs call for sizes 6-12 in 1/2 to 3 inch lengths. Check size and length before you buy.

Selecting Your Doors

Exterior doors are commonly 1-3/4" thick, not less than 80" high, and 32" to 36" wide. Exterior doors should be solid-core wood or insulated metal construction. Solid core means the space between the front and back surfaces is filled with either wood or particle board. A solid door offers more security and is less subject to warping that can be caused by humidity and differences in temperature between the indoors and outdoors.

Decide on the quantity and sizes of doors along with which way the door swings before framing begins. Be sure all framing openings for doors (and windows) are correctly dimensioned and squared. The door manufacturer provides dimensioning information, so be sure to obtain this data from your building supply dealer.

Figure 19A - Door Types

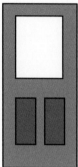   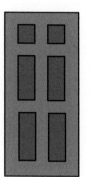 

| Two Panel/Glass | Cross Buck/Glass | Four Panel | Six Panel Colonial | Flush |

Selecting Your Windows

Most garage designs incorporate one or more windows to admit light and provide a view to the outdoors. Fixed window designs do not open but provide excellent protection against air infiltration. Operable windows include awning, double hung, casement and slider designs as shown. Casement windows usually open outward and provide excellent ventilation. Single- and double-hung windows, as their names imply, have one or two sashes that open. They provide slightly less ventilation when compared to casement designs. Awning windows are hinged at the top or bottom and open either in or out. They provide excellent airflow and are easy to clean from the exterior.

There are several different types of materials used in window manufacturing. Though wood windows require some maintenance, aluminum or vinyl require little to no maintenance.

Selection is more or less a matter of personal taste, but there might be some local code restrictions. Know the exact frame-out dimensions or rough opening sizes for the windows you selected before wall framing begins.

Figure 19B - Window Types

  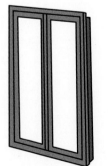 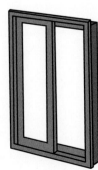 

| Awning | Double-hung | Casement | Slider | Single Unit |

Typical Garage Wall and Roof Framing Plan

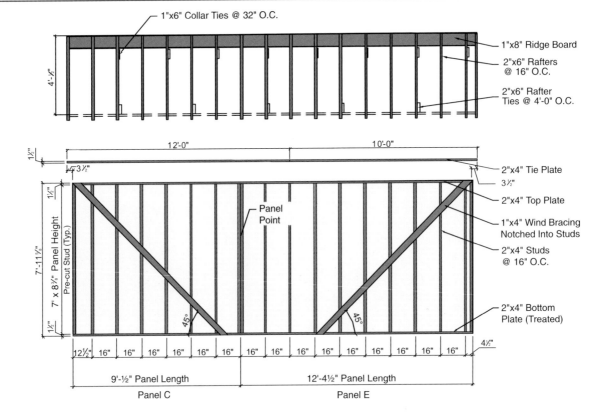

1"x6" Collar Ties @ 32" O.C.

1"x8" Ridge Board

2"x6" Rafters @ 16" O.C.

2"x6" Rafter Ties @ 4'-0" O.C.

4'-X"

12'-0"   10'-0"

1½"

3½"

2"x4" Tie Plate

3½"

2"x4" Top Plate

1½"

Panel Point

7'-11⅞"

7' x 8⅛" Panel Height Pre-cut Stud (Typ.)

1"x4" Wind Bracing Notched Into Studs

2"x4" Studs @ 16" O.C.

1½"

45°   45°

2"x4" Bottom Plate (Treated)

4½"

12½" 16" 16" 16" 16" 16" 16" 16" 16" 16" 16" 16" 16" 16" 16" 16"

9'-½" Panel Length   12'-4½" Panel Length

Panel C   Panel E

Typical Garage Floor Panel (Wall Panel System)

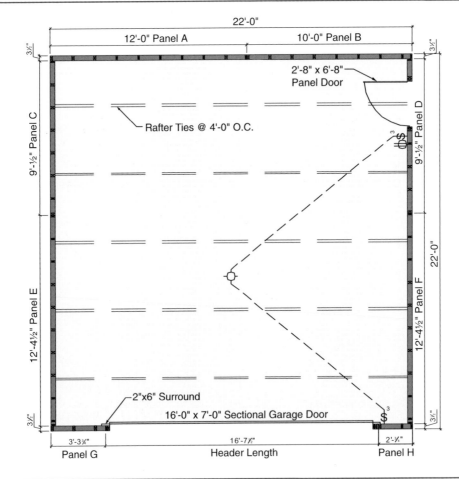

22'-0"

12'-0" Panel A   10'-0" Panel B

3½"   3½"

2'-8" x 6'-8" Panel Door

9'-½" Panel C

9'-½" Panel D

Rafter Ties @ 4'-0" O.C.

S^3

12'-4½" Panel E

12'-4½" Panel F

22'-0"

2"x6" Surround

16'-0" x 7'-0" Sectional Garage Door

3½"   3½"

S^3

3'-3¾"   16'-7½"   2'-X"

Panel G   Header Length   Panel H

Garage Wall Framing

The basic wall framing outlined on the following pages can be used for whatever roof system you choose. It is recommended you work from a professionally drawn set of plans, that are available on pages 64-157. Use the plan to determine the materials you will need and to make any special alterations to the basic framing, such as rough opening dimensions for doors and windows. You should also determine if the siding you plan to install will require three studs at the corners for nailing and if sheathing is necessary.

Wall framing includes a bottom or sole plate, evenly spaced wall studs, and a top plate. A tie plate is added to the top plate once the walls are raised. Extra studding and headers are needed at door and window openings.

In most cases, walls are built of 2x4 studs and plates with studs spaced on 16" centers. 2x6 studs can also be used with a stud spacing of 24". Bottom plates should be treated lumber to resist rot.

Some vehicles require 8' high garage doors versus a standard 7' high door. You may consider what types of vehicles will use your new garage. If 8' doors are required you will need to substitute 9' studs instead of 8' studs.

Set Bottom Plate

The bottom plate rests on the foundation walls, flush with the outside edge of each wall. Snap chalk lines to set the plate's inner edge and check for squareness by measuring the diagonals. If anchor bolts were used, position the bottom plates against the anchor bolts and mark off the hole locations. When using standard 1/2" diameter anchor bolts, drill 3/4" holes at these locations. Temporarily install bottom plates over the anchor bolts to check positioning.

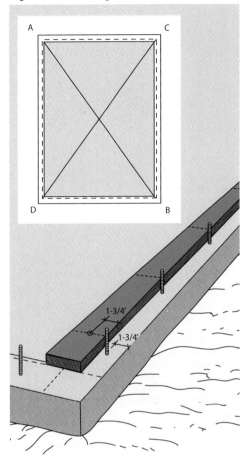

Figure 21A - Setting Bottom Plates

Constructing the Basic Wall Frame

To begin, cut both the top and bottom plates to length. In most cases, you will need more than one piece of lumber for each plate. So locate the joints at stud centers and offset joints between top and bottom plates by at least 4'.

Lay the top plate against the bottom plate on the slab as illustrated below. Beginning at one end, measure in 15-1/4" and draw a line across both plates. Measure out farther along the plates an additional distance of 1-1/2" from this line, and draw a second line. The first interior stud will be placed between these lines.

From these lines, advance 16" at a time, drawing new lines, until you reach the far end of the plates. Each set of lines will outline the placement of a stud, with all studs evenly spaced at 16" on center. If you are using studs on 24" centers, the first measurement in from the edge would be 23-1/4".

Figure 21B - Measuring Bottom Plates

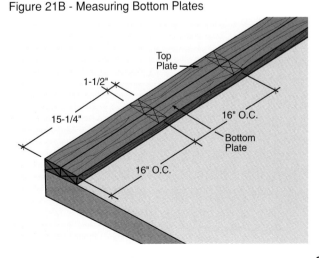

Constructing the Basic Wall Frame

Assembling the Pieces

Unless you are using precut studs, the next step is to measure and cut the wall studs to exact length. Position the plates apart on the slab and turn them on edge with stud marking toward the center. Place the studs between the lines and nail them through each plate with two 16d common nails.

Framing Corners

Where walls meet, you might need extra studs to handle the corner tie to the adjacent wall. These extra studs should be added to the ends of the longer two of the four walls. The exact positioning of these extra corner studs is shown at the bottom of page 25.

Figure 22 - Assembling the Walls

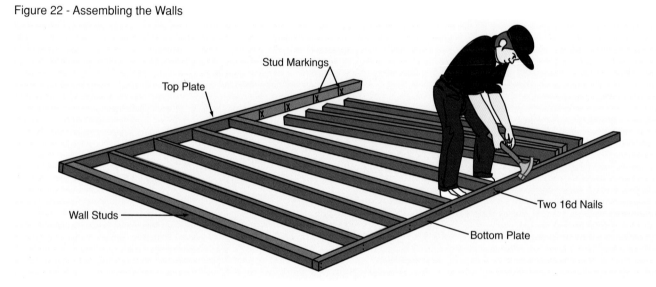

Door and Window Framing

At door and window openings there is no stud support, so a header is required. Door and window headers can be constructed either from 4x dimensional lumber, veneer laminate lumber also known as engineered lumber, or two lengths of 2x material on edge with a 1/2" piece of plywood sandwiched between them. When you are constructing a built-up header from doubled-up 2x material, the plywood makes the header the same 3-1/2" width as the studs.

Headers are always installed on edge as shown in Figure 23A. Consult the chart below to determine the header size required for a given span.

The spaces above door openings and above and below windows are framed with cripple studs spaced 16" on center. Study the illustrations in Figure 23B to become familiar with the king and trimmer stud locations used in framing doors and windows.

The rough framed door should be 1-1/2" higher than the usual 80" actual door height and 2-1/2" wider than the door to account for door jamb material. When the 1-1/2" bottom plate is cut from the opening, this adds the needed 1-1/2" in extra height.

In addition to cripple studs, king studs, and trimmer studs, window framing also uses a rough sill to support the window. Headers should be set at the same time as the door headers. Two cripple studs may be required on each side for openings greater than 8'-0". Consult the manufacturer's instructions for a suggested roughout opening to accommodate a given window.

Header Size (4x or built-up 2x)	Maximum Span (feet)
4 x 4	4
4 x 6	6
4 x 8	8
4 x 10	10
4 x 12	12

Door and Window Framing

Header Assembly

Nail two pieces of 2xs and plywood to the length between king studs with 16d nails spaced 16" apart along both top and bottom edges as shown in Figure 23A.

Figure 23A - Header Assembly

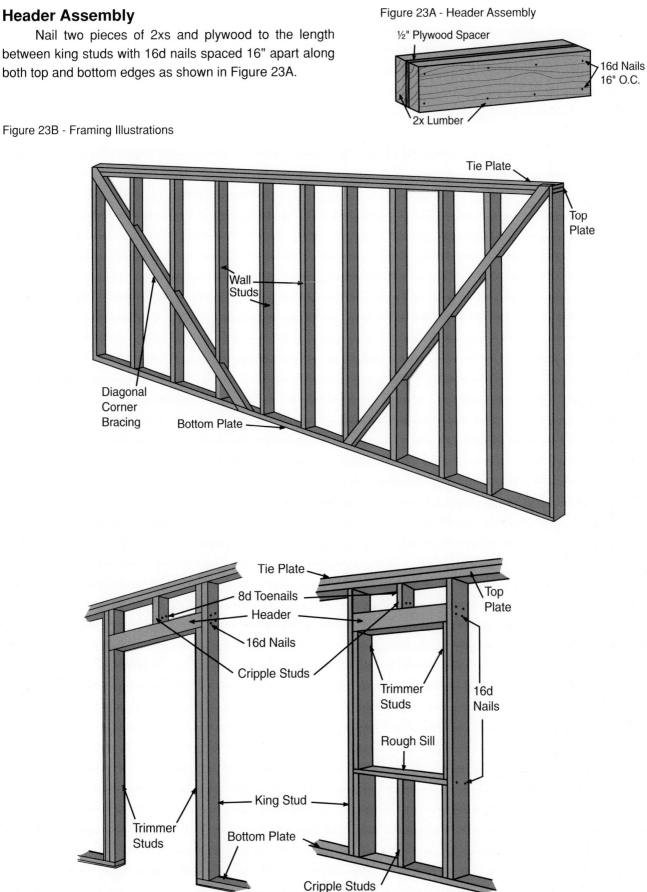

½" Plywood Spacer

16d Nails 16" O.C.

2x Lumber

Figure 23B - Framing Illustrations

Tie Plate

Top Plate

Wall Studs

Diagonal Corner Bracing

Bottom Plate

Tie Plate

8d Toenails

Header

16d Nails

Cripple Studs

Top Plate

Trimmer Studs

16d Nails

Rough Sill

King Stud

Trimmer Studs

Bottom Plate

Cripple Studs

Diagonal Bracing

Structures with plywood siding normally do not require bracing, but all others do. The three most commonly used types of bracing are wooden "let-in" bracing made of 1x4 stock, metal strap bracing and plywood sheathing at corners.

Let-In Bracing

This type of wooden bracing runs from the top outside corners of the wall to the bottom center of the wall. It forms a V-shaped configuration as shown on Figure 23B. These braces are set into notched studs and are prepared while the wall frame is still lying on the slab. Lay the 1x4 on the frame with one end at a top corner and the other end as far out on the bottom plate as possible without running into any door or window opening. Mark the underside of the brace where it overhangs the top and bottom plates to determine the angle at which the plates cross. Also mark both sides of the studs and plates at each point the brace crosses them. Notch the studs at these locations by making repeated cuts with your circular saw. Use a hammer and wood chisel to knock out any stubborn chips. Trim the ends of the 1x4 and put the brace in place. Hold it in place with a single nail until the wall is raised and plumbed. Then nail the brace with 8d nails wherever it crosses a plate or stud.

Metal Strap Bracing

Commonly available in 10' to 12' lengths, this type of bracing is nailed to the outside of the studded walls after they are raised, square, and plumb. Metal bracing is thin enough not to obstruct the exterior wall sheathing. The straps have predrilled holes every 2" sized to accept an 8d nail. Strap bracing must always be installed in crossed pairs, similar to a large X design.

Plywood Corner Bracing

If wall sheathing is used, you may substitute 48" wide structural plywood sheathing at corners for wood let-ins or metal bracing. See nailing schedule for proper nailing conditions when using wood sheathing.

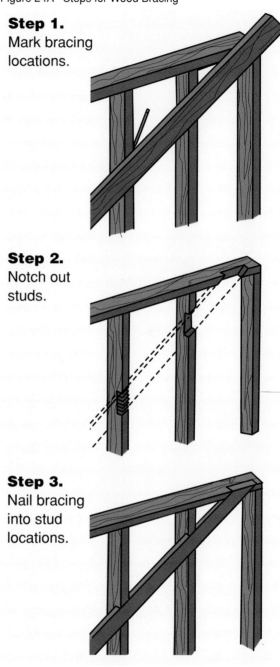

Figure 24A - Steps for Wood Bracing

Step 1. Mark bracing locations.

Step 2. Notch out studs.

Step 3. Nail bracing into stud locations.

Figure 24B - Alternate Metal Strap

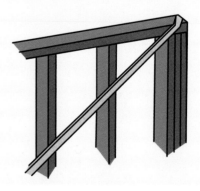

Raising the Walls

Most walls can be raised by hand if enough help is available on the job site. It is advisable to have one person for every 10' of wall for the lifting operation.

The order in which walls are framed and raised can vary from job to job, but in general, the longer exterior walls are framed first. The shorter exterior walls are then raised and the corners are nailed together.

Once the first wall is framed out, there are only a few short steps until it is up and standing. If you are raising a wall on a slab, slide the wall along the slab until the bottom plate lies near the anchor bolt at the floor's edge. If you are raising a wall on a wood floor, you might want to tack some scrap lumber along the floor rim joists to prevent the wall from slipping over the edge. To raise the wall have your workers grip it at the top plate in unison and work their hands beneath the plate. Now everyone walks down the wall until it is in the upright position. On a slab you need to slip the bottom plate in place over the anchor bolts as you tilt the wall up.

To brace the wall, tack 2x4 braces to the wall studs, one at each end and one in the middle if the wall is particularly long. Tie these braces into stakes driven firmly into the ground or tack them to the wood floor rim joists if appropriate. Secure the wall by using washers and nuts if you have anchor bolts or tack the bottom plate to the wood floor. Do not securely nail the bottom plate to the floor until you are certain that the walls are in proper alignment.

To check alignment, use a carpenter's level to check the wall for plumb along both end studs on adjacent faces. If the wall is out of plumb, loosen that brace, align the wall, and secure the brace again. If an end stud is warped, bridge the warp with a straight board. When both ends are plumb, adjust the middle.

Nailing Schedule for Structural Members

Description of Building Materials	Number & Type of Fastener	Spacing of Fasteners
Top or sole plate to stud, end nail	2-16d	-
Stud to sole plate, toenail	4-8d or 3-16d	
Doubled studs, face nail	16d	24" O.C.
Doubled top plates, face nail	16d	16" O.C.
Top plates, taps and intersections, face nail	2-16d	-
Continued header, two pieces	16d	16" O.C. along each edge
Ceiling joists to plate, toenail	2-16d	-
Continuous header to stud, toenail	4-8d	-
Ceiling joist, taps over partitions, face nail	3-16d	-
Ceiling joist to parallel rafters, face nail	3-16d	-
Rafter to plate, toe nail	2-16d	-
1" brace to each stud and plate, face nail	2-8d	-
Built-up corner studs	16d	30" O.C.
Built-up girder and beams	16d	32" O.C. at top & bottom & staggered 2-20d at ends & at each splice
Roof rafters to ridge, valley or hip rafters, toenail	4-16d	-
Face nail	3-16d	-
Collar ties to rafters, face nail	3-8d	-

Description of Building Materials	Description of Fasteners	Spacing of Fasteners
Roof and wall sheathing to frame		
1/2 inch to 5/16 inch roof & wall sheathing to frame	6d	6" edges 12" intermediate supports
Other wall sheathing		
1/2 inch fiberboard sheathing	1 1/2" galvanized roofing nail 6d common nail	3" edges 6" intermediate supports

Figure 25 - To raise the wall, have your workers grip it at the top plate in unison and work their hands beneath the plate. Now everyone walks down the wall until it is in the upright position. To check alignment, use a carpenter's level.

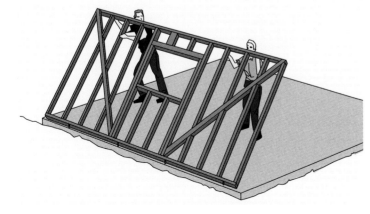

Leveling and Corner Details

Once raised, the wall should also be checked for levelness. If needed, it can be shimmed level using tapered cedar shingles driven between the foundation and the bottom plate. Once the wall is plumb and level, tighten the anchor nuts to their final tightness or on wooden floors nail two 16d common nails between each stud. Do not nail the bottom plate in a door opening since this section must be cut out for the door.

At corners, nail through the end walls into the stud using 16d common nails staggered every 12". When the walls are up, you can add the 2x4 tie plates to the top plates on each wall. These tie plates lap over onto adjacent walls to interlock the walls and give added strength to the structure.

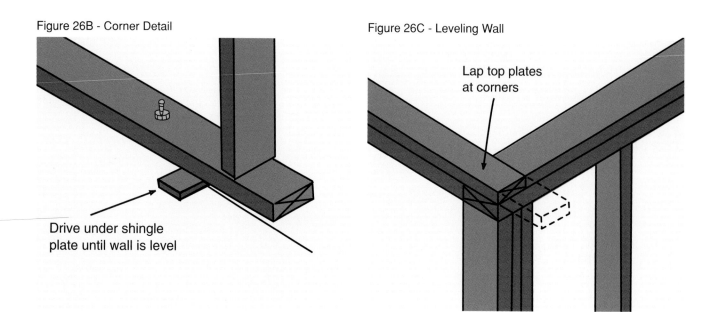

Figure 26B - Corner Detail

Drive under shingle plate until wall is level

Figure 26C - Leveling Wall

Lap top plates at corners

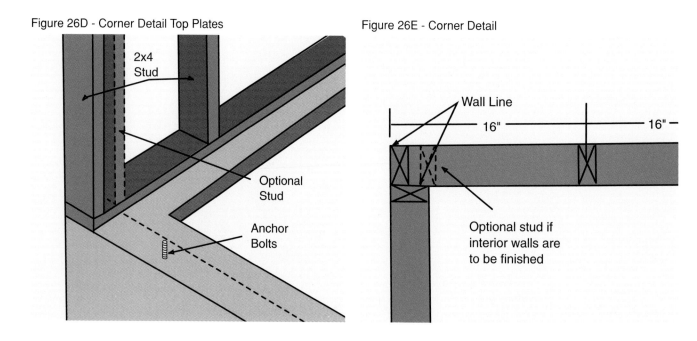

Figure 26D - Corner Detail Top Plates

2x4 Stud

Optional Stud

Anchor Bolts

Figure 26E - Corner Detail

Wall Line

16"

16"

Optional stud if interior walls are to be finished

Framing with Metal Fasteners

When undertaking a large-scale construction project, such as your garage, you may find it easier to use a variety of metal fasteners and supports to tie beams together, hang joists, support posts, or tie rafters. These metal fasteners come in different sizes to accommodate all sizes of structural lumber, and most hardware stores carry a large selection. In some areas, use of metal fasteners is optional, but in other regions where hurricanes and high wind factors are a problem, special connectors may be required by the building code. While metal framing connectors will add some additional expense to your project, they will save you time and create a more durable garage.

Figure 27C - Framing Anchors

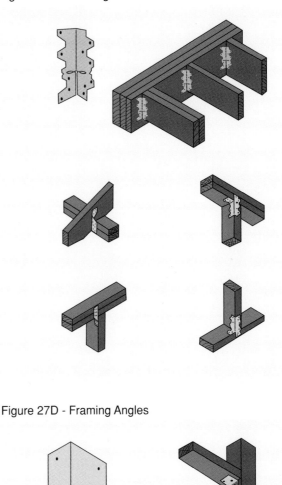

Figure 27A - Joist Hangers

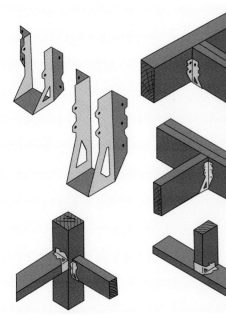

Figure 27D - Framing Angles

Figure 27B - Post Anchors

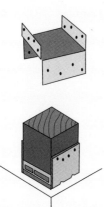

Figure 27E - Nail-On Plates

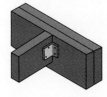

Roof Framing

There are two major types of roof framing. One type is the use of pre-engineered roof trusses, which are less time consuming than conventional rafters or stick framing. Check with your local lumberyard for availability in your area. Generally rafters are 2x6s or 2x8s, depending on span, spacing, load and roof slope, and are installed on 16-inch or 24-inch centers. Check with your local building office for help with these variables. At the peak, rafter boards butt against a central ridge board. The ridge board is generally made up of 2x lumber and is one size wider than the rafter lumber. For example, use 2x8 ridge board if the rafters are 2x6s, 2x10 ridge board with 2x8s, and so on. Slope, or pitch, is referred to in terms of **unit rise** in **unit run**. **Unit run** is fixed at 12 inches. **Unit rise** is the slope over those 12". A rise of 4" over 12" is a slope of 4" in 12".

Cutting the Rafters

A **common rafter** has three cuts: the **plumb cut** to form the angle where the rafter meets the ridge board, the **bird's mouth notch** to fit the top plate, and the **tail** at the end of the overhang. Most professionally prepared plans, such as those offered at the end of this manual, often have a template or diagram for a master or "pattern" rafter. Cut two rafters off the master and check them for accuracy before cutting the others. Use a steel carpenter's square to mark the cuts.

Raising the Roof

With ridge board and rafters cut, you can raise the roof. You'll need three people. Nail an upright 2x4 for each of the end rafters flush against the middle of the end top plate. One person then lines up one end rafter with the end of the side top plate and ties it in with three 16d nails. The second raises and holds it at the correct slope against one of the 2x4s, while the third nails the two together. Do the same with the opposite end rafter, then align the ridge board between the top of the rafters and tie it with three 16d nails through each rafter. The ridge board must be level, and the rafter ends must be flush with the sides of the ridge board. Repeat the process at the opposite end for a single-piece ridge board; for a two-piece ridge board, tie the rafters to the last spacing mark at the opposite end.

Figure 28 - Making Rafter Patterns

For those of us not familiar with a square, lay out the initial pair of rafters on the slab. Snap chalk lines to represent the bottom of the rafters and the plate line. Use the rise in 12" to establish the angle (for example, 4" in 12"). If they fit, use them as patterns for all other rafters.

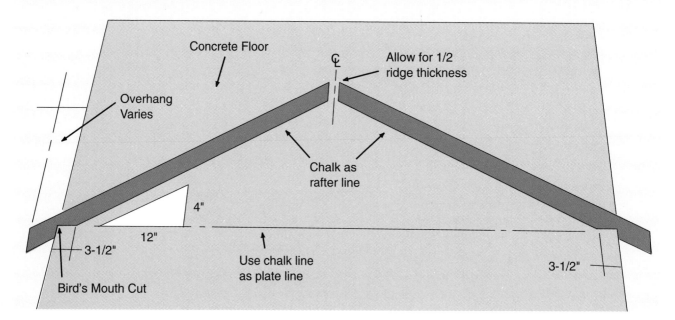

Roof Framing

Figure 29A - Rafter Cuts

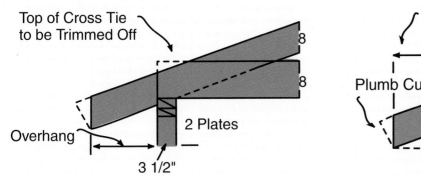

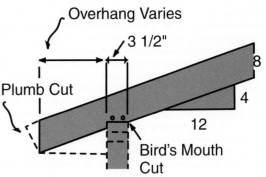

Leveling and Bracing

Make sure the end rafters are plumb, and the ridge board is level and centered mid-span, then attach a diagonal brace between the ridge board and the 2x4 nailed to the top plate. Run the remaining rafters in pairs, attaching them to the ridge board first, then to the top plate. If a second ridge board is used, the process is repeated from the opposite end of the building. The junction of the ridge boards must be covered by two rafters. Use three 16d nails to tie rafters to rafter ties (joists) and cut ties to match the slope of the rafters.

Be sure to add collar ties and hangers before removing any shoring or bracing. Blocks can be needed on the eaves for extended overhangs.

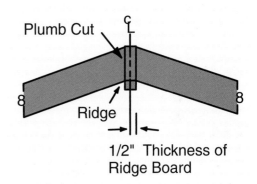

Figure 29B - Typical Garage Wall Section

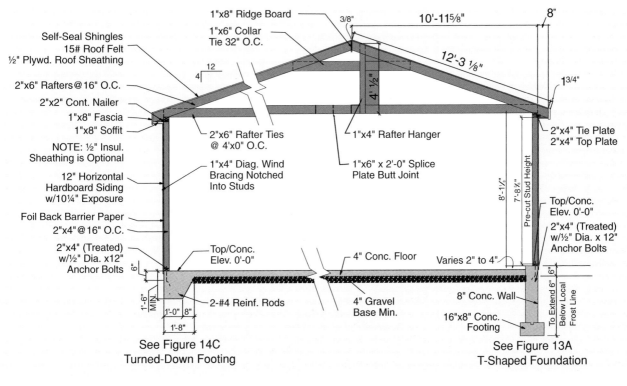

See Figure 14C
Turned-Down Footing

See Figure 13A
T-Shaped Foundation

Roof Framing

As mentioned earlier, metal fasteners provide the strength nails alone cannot provide. They also avoid the irritation of watching angled nails split the lumber which you have so carefully cut and fitted. Certain metal connectors allow the rafter to rest directly on the tie or top plate and eliminate the difficult and time-consuming bird's mouth cut.

Other connectors are designed to join the rafter to the ridge board without toenailing. As illustrated, many different types of metal connectors are available for roof framing work. While metal roof framing connectors will add some additional expense to your project, they will save you time and create a more durable garage.

Figure 30A - Typical Rafter Cutting Diagram

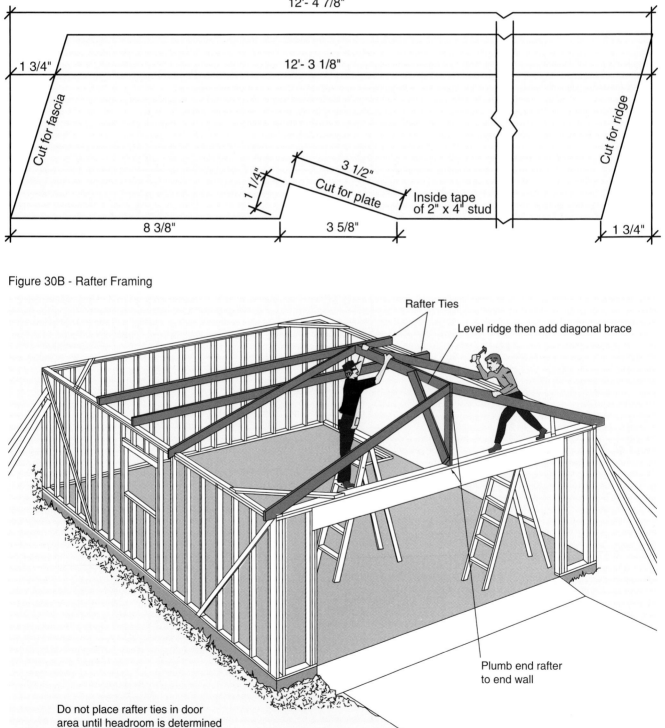

Figure 30B - Rafter Framing

Roof Framing

Figure 31 - Metal Roof Framing Connectors

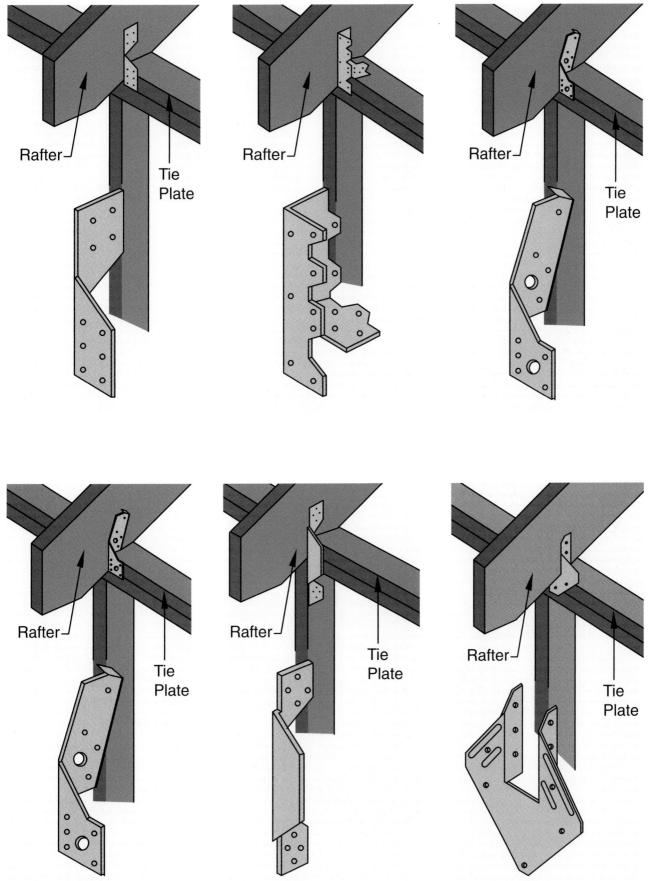

Figure 31 - Metal Roof Framing Connectors

Roof Framing

Roof Trusses

Pre-engineered trusses are often available from local lumber dealers. They are designed to span the full width of a structure from one exterior wall to the other. This leaves a large room free of supports. The use of preassembled trusses speeds the erection of the roof. Be certain to obtain your trusses from a reliable source who will custom design and build them to your needs. Refer to truss manufacturer's installation and bracing requirements prior to erecting trusses.

Erecting Trusses

It is advisable to have at least two other persons assisting you when erecting roof trusses. Have all walls securely braced. The steps to follow are:

1. With one person at each side wall of the structure and one at the center, place the trusses onto the top plate of the outside walls, upside down, Figure 32A.
2. Move the first gable end truss into position at the end of the building and swing it up into position with the man in the center working from the ground with a pole to push the center up, Figure 32B.
3. Center truss between side walls. Plumb truss and temporarily toenail in place. Brace gable truss down to ground stake to keep it plumb.
4. Repeat Step 3 at opposite gable end.
5. Place nails at peak of each gable truss. Run a string line from one end to the other and draw tight.
6. Tilt up one truss at a time. Be sure that the peak is exactly under string line. Space truss 24" apart measured from center to center. Laterally brace all trusses to keep them from tipping over. A 2x nailed to the top of each truss after it is plumb will keep them in line until the roof sheathing is applied, Figure 32C.
7. Remove temporary bracing from the top of the trusses only after roof sheathing has been applied. Note: Refer to truss manufacturing specifications for truss bracing.
8. Fasten each truss to the top plate using metal framing anchors, use one at each end of the truss. (See page 31).
9. Often construction blueprints call for a different size rafter than the top chord of trusses. If this is so, adjust the trim boards to accommodate the variance.

Figure 32A

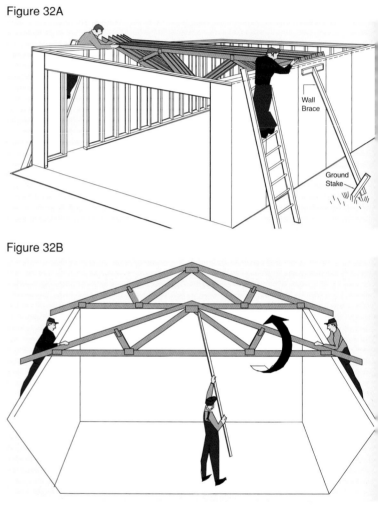

Figure 32B

Figure 32C

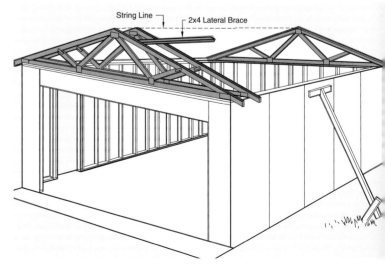

Roof Framing

Roof Sheathing

Using 4'x8' plywood panels covers large roof areas quickly, although 1x8s laid up tightly can also be used. The required thickness of the sheathing will vary with rafter spacing and local building code requirements. Generally, the wider the rafters are spaced, the thicker the sheathing needs to be.

Stagger the sheathing, starting at the bottom, so that the end joints of adjacent sheets fall on different rafters. It is advisable to use plywood clips to help secure plywood together. Space 8d nails 6" apart at sheet ends, and 12" on center at intermediate rafters. If gable eaves have an overhang, extend the sheathing to cover it.

Figure 33A - Garage Door Opener

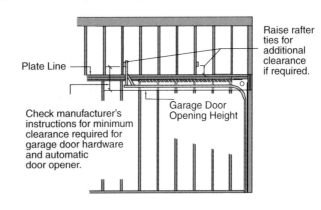

Note: Check garage door hardware and opener instructions before nailing rafter ties in place. Minimum clearance requirements between the top of the door opening and the bottom of the ties might require that the ties be set off of the top plate. See Figure 33A.

Note: Before roof sheathing is in place, determine garage door hardware headroom and then add rafter ties to clear the hardware.

Figure 33B - Roofing Diagram

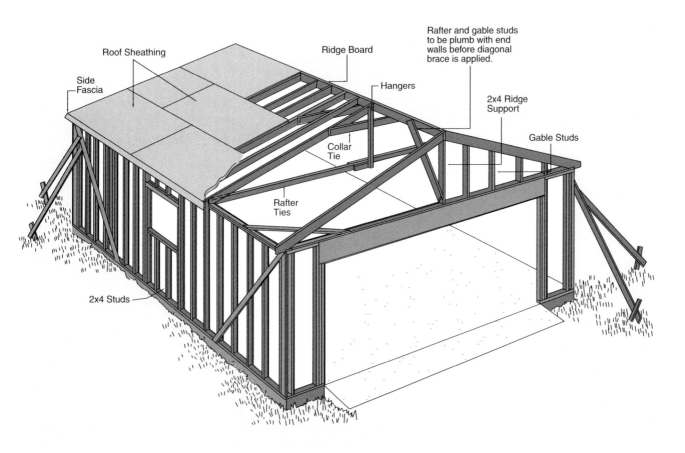

Roof Framing

Variations of the Roof Cornice

Whatever type of roof you decide to construct, your building will have a roof overhang to protect the top of the side walls from moisture penetration. This overhang is generally known as the roof cornice. The cornice can also serve to provide ventilation and protection from the hot overhead rays of the sun on the sidewalls. As a general rule of thumb, warmer climates tend to favor longer overhangs that offer greater shading.

An open cornice is illustrated in Figure 34A. The overhang can extend up to 24" from the edge of the building. You have the option of adding a frieze board to the rafter ends or leaving the rafter ends exposed. Remember that when you create an exposed overhang, the roof sheathing is visible from underneath. Painting or staining the sheathing can improve its appearance.

Figure 34B represents a closed cornice. Make a seat cut on the rafter at the top plate. Cut the rafter ends flush and vertical with the top plate. Bring the siding all the way up to the rafters and finish off the cornice with a trim piece that covers the slightly exposed roof sheathing.

Two variations of the boxed cornice are shown in Figures 34C and 34D. A fascia board at the rafter ends is essential for any style of boxed cornice. Figure 34C demonstrates the sloping soffit design where the rafters are used to directly attach the soffit board. Nail a 1x fascia board to the square cut rafter ends. Another frieze board covers the end portion of the soffit where it meets the wall siding.

Figure 34D portrays the level soffit design that requires 2x4 horizontal lookouts facenailed at the rafter ends and toenailed to wall siding. Level soffits generally extend no more than 12"-15" from the building wall. The lookouts help to frame the soffit construction.

Proper ventilation is essential for the boxed cornice. Install soffit vents (typically 4"x8") at regular intervals along the soffit between the lookouts. Be sure to install the screened vents or you will have unintentionally created a birdhouse wherever you have an unscreened vent!

Ventilation

If you plan to use your garage as a work area or local codes require ventilation, consider installing either gable end vents or roof vents. Vents help to reduce interior temperatures during the summer months. Gable end vents should be installed at both gable ends of your roof to promote cross-ventilation.

The number of roof vents you will install depends upon the cubic footage of your building. Simply create a box frame between roof rafters and install the vent according to the manufacturer's instructions. Don't forget to flash and then caulk the vent after you have installed the roof sheathing and shingles.

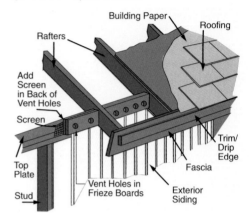

Figure 34A - Open Cornice

Figure 34B - Closed Cornice

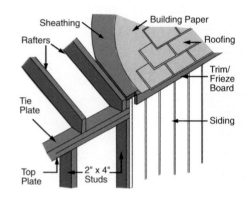

Figure 34C - Boxed Cornice/Sloping Soffit

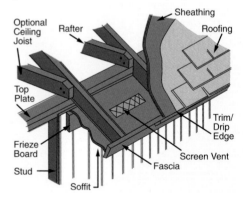

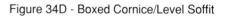

Figure 34D - Boxed Cornice/Level Soffit

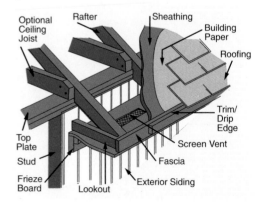

Hip Roof Framing

Rafter lengths require some paperwork on hip roofs. Layout a plan view of the roof on graph paper as shown in Figure 35C. The larger the scale, the greater the accuracy, so use a minimum 1" to 1' scale.

Calculating Rafter Lengths

To determine rafter lengths, draw horizontal line A–B (Figure 35B). Locate A' by projecting up the scale height of the roof slope. A line between A' and B will give the angle for plumb and tail cuts on common and jack rafters, as well as common rafter length (except for the additional length at top for cutting angle). Lay hip roof out similarly: horizontal line A–C, and A'–C for hip length, allow enough length for angle cut.

For jack rafter lengths, lay out points X, Y, Z, and so on, along A–B and project up to A'–B. In addition to the plumb, tail, and bird's mouth cuts, jack rafters must also be cut to 45 degrees across the narrow width (Figure 35A) to line up with the hip rafter.

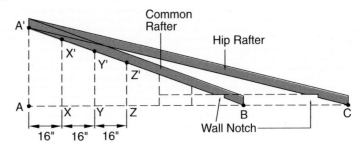

Figure 35B - Determining Rafter Lengths

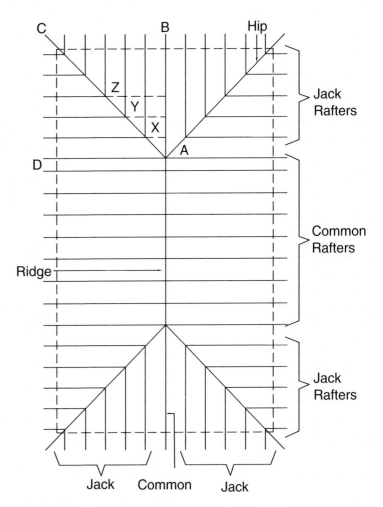

Figure 35C - Hip Roof Layout

Figure 35A - Jack Rafter Cut

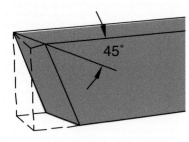

Jack Rafter Schedule																	
Position	A	A'	B	B'	C	C'	D	D'	E	E'	F	F'	G	G'	H	J
Overall Length = "x"	12'- 1"	13'- 5⅞"	10'- 8⅛"	12'- 1"	9'- 3¼"	10'- 8⅛"	7'- 10⅜"	9'- 3¼"	6'- 5½"	7'- 10⅜"	5'- 0⅝"	6'- 5½"	3'- 7¾"	5'- 0⅝"	2'- 2⅞"	4'- 6"
No. Required @45° Bevel	3	1	3	1	3	1	3	1	3	1	3	1	3	1	4	1
No. Required @ Reverse 45° B	3	1	3	1	3	1	3	1	3	1	3	1	3	1	4	1

Hip Roof Framing

Figure 36A - Rafter Peak Detail

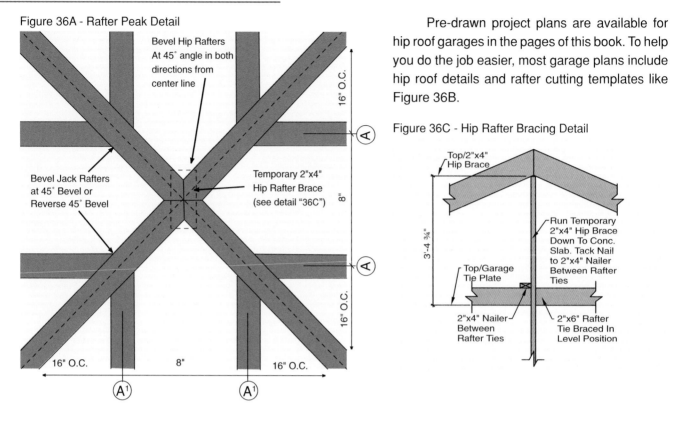

Bevel Hip Rafters At 45° angle in both directions from center line

Bevel Jack Rafters at 45° Bevel or Reverse 45° Bevel

Temporary 2"x4" Hip Rafter Brace (see detail "36C")

16" O.C.

8"

16" O.C.

16" O.C.

8"

16" O.C.

Pre-drawn project plans are available for hip roof garages in the pages of this book. To help you do the job easier, most garage plans include hip roof details and rafter cutting templates like Figure 36B.

Figure 36C - Hip Rafter Bracing Detail

Top/2"x4" Hip Brace

Run Temporary 2"x4" Hip Brace Down To Conc. Slab. Tack Nail to 2"x4" Nailer Between Rafter Ties

Top/Garage Tie Plate

3'-4 ¾"

2"x4" Nailer Between Rafter Ties

2"x6" Rafter Tie Braced In Level Position

Figure 36B - Typical Hip Rafter Cutting Templates

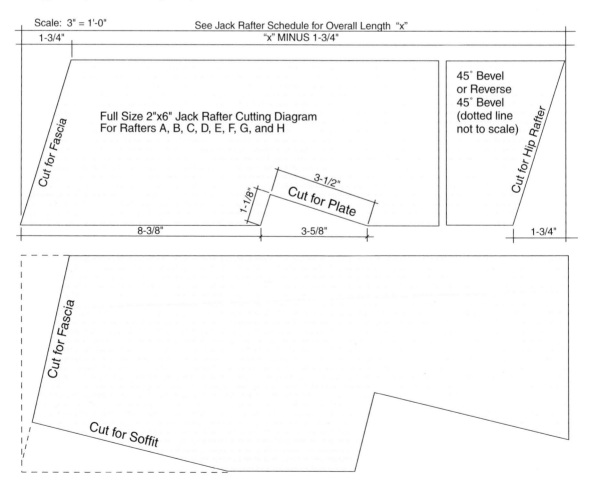

Scale: 3" = 1'-0"

See Jack Rafter Schedule for Overall Length "x"

1-3/4"

"x" MINUS 1-3/4"

Cut for Fascia

Full Size 2"x6" Jack Rafter Cutting Diagram For Rafters A, B, C, D, E, F, G, and H

45° Bevel or Reverse 45° Bevel (dotted line not to scale)

Cut for Hip Rafter

3-1/2"

1-1/8"

Cut for Plate

8-3/8"

3-5/8"

1-3/4"

Cut for Fascia

Cut for Soffit

Hip Roof Framing

Erecting a Hip Roof

To erect the hip roof, begin with the common rafters along the ridge (Figure 37A), or erect four common rafters if the building is square. Nail up rafter ties as well (Figure 37B). Before nailing the rafter ties in position, it is strongly suggested that you check for proper clearance for any planned garage door and garage door opener. Most garage doors require a minimum clearance between the top of the garage door opening and the bottom of the rafter ties. The door and opener manufacturer provides these clearances and you can check them with your building supplier. To gain the clearance required, it might be necessary to set the rafter ties off the top and tie plate. See Figure 33A.

Nail hip rafters to corners, and use a temporary brace to create a slight crown in them (Figure 37B). Next, nail up jack rafters in opposing pairs connected to rafter ties. Use just one nail in each until all are in place, then adjust them to straighten the hip rafter and nail them in permanently.

Figure 37A - Hip Roof Peak Detail

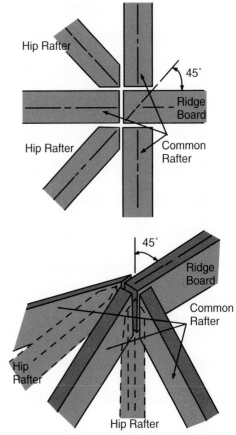

Figure 37B - Hip Roof Framing

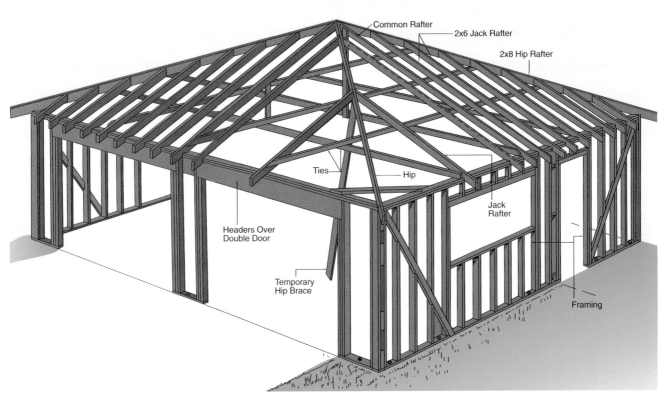

Hip Roof Framing

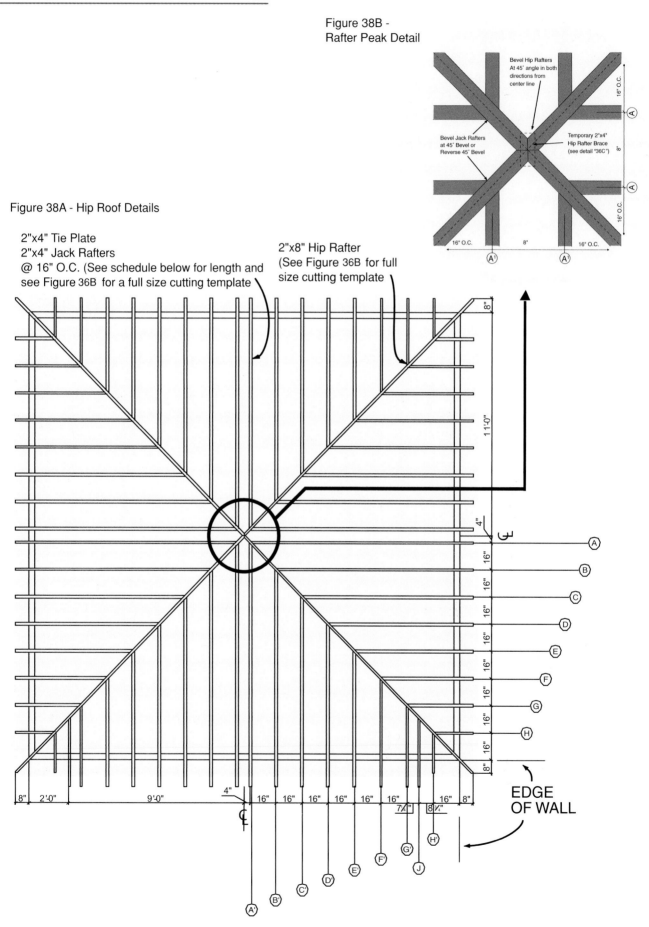

Figure 38B -
Rafter Peak Detail

Bevel Hip Rafters
At 45° angle in both
directions from
center line

Bevel Jack Rafters
at 45° Bevel or
Reverse 45° Bevel

Temporary 2"x4"
Hip Rafter Brace
(see detail "36C")

16" O.C.

8"

16" O.C.

16" O.C.

8"

16" O.C.

Figure 38A - Hip Roof Details

2"x4" Tie Plate
2"x4" Jack Rafters
@ 16" O.C. (See schedule below for length and
see Figure 36B for a full size cutting template

2"x8" Hip Rafter
(See Figure 36B for full
size cutting template

EDGE
OF WALL

Overhang Details

Before applying trim, know the nailing requirements of the siding you select. Some siding will have trim applied over the siding, but other siding will butt against trim and require extra blocking at the edges. After the roof sheathing is on but before you install the fascia and rake boards, add soffit nailers if required. Use the longest fascia boards on the longest walls. Join all ends over the center of a rafter or nailer.

Consult Figures 39A to 39F below. At the gable end, extend the fascia (or rake board) along the edge of the roof sheathing and rafter. At the top, cut the end to the angle of the rafter and butt at the center. Be sure to prime coat both ends before butting. At the lower end, let the front rake fascia extend beyond the side fascia, then cut the ends to line up with the side fascia.

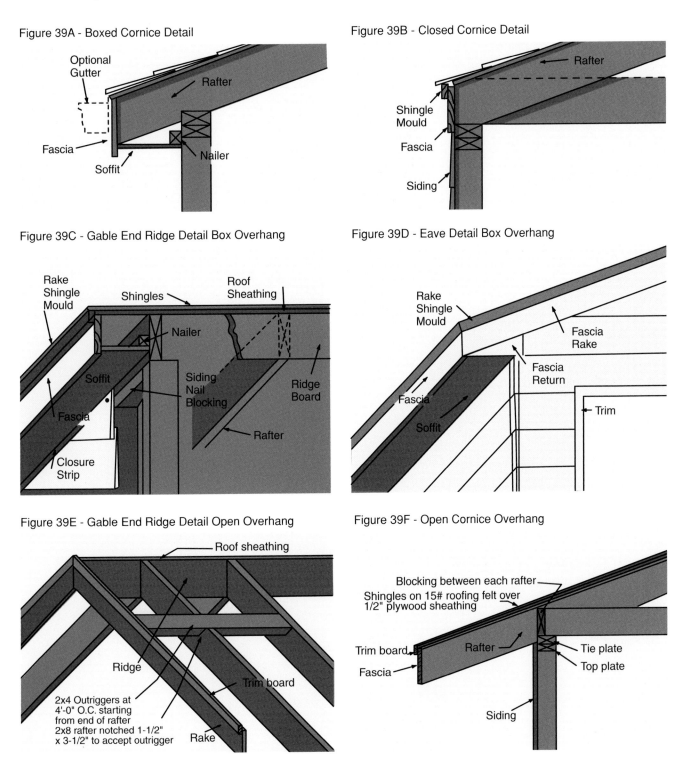

Figure 39A - Boxed Cornice Detail

Figure 39B - Closed Cornice Detail

Figure 39C - Gable End Ridge Detail Box Overhang

Figure 39D - Eave Detail Box Overhang

Figure 39E - Gable End Ridge Detail Open Overhang

Figure 39F - Open Cornice Overhang

Trim Details

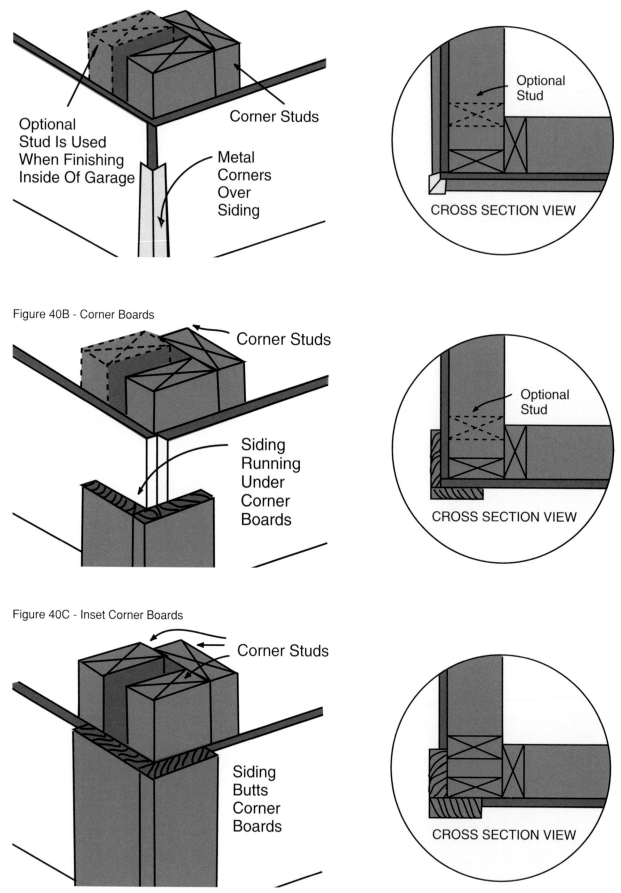

Figure 40A - Corner Tins

Optional Stud Is Used When Finishing Inside Of Garage

Corner Studs

Metal Corners Over Siding

Optional Stud

CROSS SECTION VIEW

Figure 40B - Corner Boards

Corner Studs

Siding Running Under Corner Boards

Optional Stud

CROSS SECTION VIEW

Figure 40C - Inset Corner Boards

Corner Studs

Siding Butts Corner Boards

CROSS SECTION VIEW

Trim Details

Window and Door Trim

Trim out door(s) as detailed on your garage plan. Because of the great variety in window manufacturing, it is best to study the window manufacturer's details before framing and trimming them. The service door to your garage can be ordered as a prehung door complete with threshold and side and head jambs. See Figures 41A-41C for construction details on trimming on-site window and door jambs.

Garage Door Trim

Nail overhead door jambs to the cripple studs and the header according to the directions given by the garage door manufacturer. The correct installation of garage door hardware, torsion springs, and trim is critical to the safe, smooth operation of the door. This is one phase of construction where we strongly recommend the work be completed by a professional installer.

Note: Window and door jambs will move out 1/2" if 1/2" wall sheathing is used. If metal sash is used, see manufacturer's instructions before framing opening.

Figure 41B - Door Detail

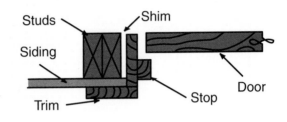

Figure 41C - Window Detail

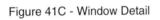

Figure 41A - Door Detail

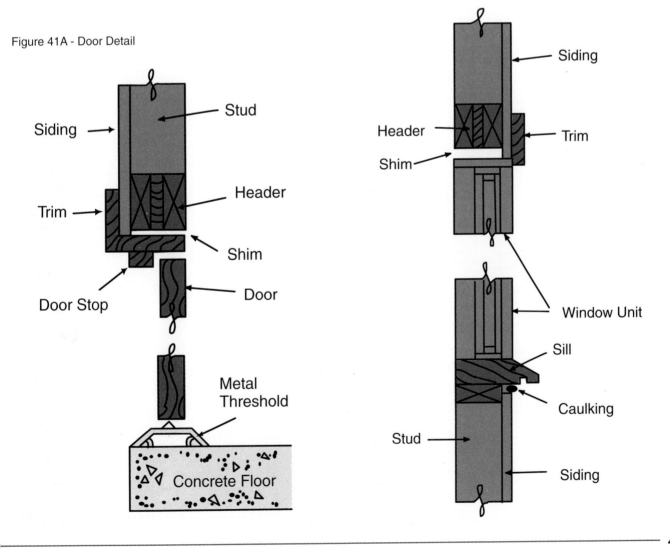

Roof Shingles

Once the roof sheathing, cornice trim, and fascia boards are in place, the roof shingles can be applied. See shingle manufacturer's instructions on bundles. Shingles, chosen to harmonize with the home, are most popular. Square butt shingles are 36" x 12" in size, have three tabs, and are normally laid with 5" exposed to the weather (Figure 42A). Start with 15# asphalt felt paper at the bottom edge of the roof. Lap each course 2". After it is on, apply a starter course of shingles (shingles turned upside down), lapping over the eave and rake fascia 1/2" to provide a drip edge. Use four nails to each shingle: apply a ridge cap at top, which is made by cutting a shingle into thirds (Figure 42B). Start at one end of the ridge and fasten with two nails to a shingle 5" exposure. Cut shingles with a utility knife. Metal drip edges are used in some locales.

When shingling a hip roof, a little more cutting is required. Use the hatchet gauge to give each hip shingle a 5" exposure.

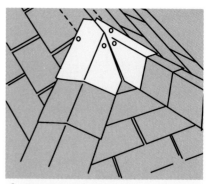

1. Trim the last hip shingles so that they meet smoothly.

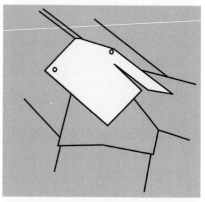

2. Cut 1st ridge shingle 4" up center; Nail over end of ridge.

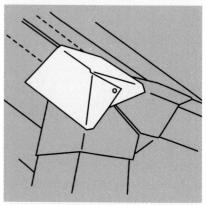

3. Fold split ends over hips and nail; Cover nails with roofing cement.

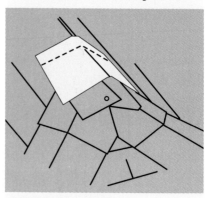

4. First ridge shingle.

Figure 42A - Laying Shingles

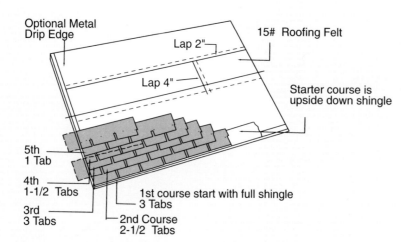

Optional Metal Drip Edge

15# Roofing Felt

Lap 2"

Lap 4"

Starter course is upside down shingle

5th 1 Tab

4th 1-1/2 Tabs

3rd 3 Tabs

2nd Course 2-1/2 Tabs

1st course start with full shingle 3 Tabs

Figure 42B - Cutting Shingles

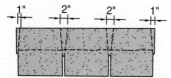

1" 2" 2" 1"

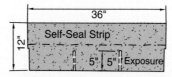

36"

12"

Self-Seal Strip

5" 5" Exposure

To cut a shingle, score a line with your utility knife, then bend and snap off the piece. Make 3 hip or ridge shingles from one shingle.

Tab shingles are always applied so that full tab is centered over a slot below. If length of roof requires a narrow piece to finish first course, start the second row with piece of same width. Continue alternating narrow pieces in each succeeding row.

Figure 42C - Applying Ridge Cap

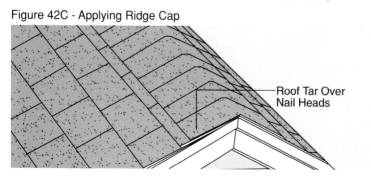

Roof Tar Over Nail Heads

Siding

Applying Vertical Panel Siding

Before starting construction, select the siding and determine the need for wall sheathing. Wall sheathing requirements are determined by the stud spacing, the width of the door and window jambs, and the application of the trim (See Figure 43A).

A commonplace and inexpensive siding for garages, T1-11 exterior siding, does not require wall sheathing and adds structural strength. Of course you should attempt to harmonize your garage siding with your home's exterior. When you install vertical panel siding, nail 6d galvanized nails every 4"-6" at the edges of the panel and every 8"-12" inside the panel. You might be able to obtain siding nails that match the siding and thus eliminate painting both the siding and nails. If you have to add a panel above the bottom panel, use Z-bar flashing between the panels (See Figure 43C). Leave a 1/4" gap around door and window openings when cutting siding to facilitate fitting.

When plywood sheathing is used, diagonal corner bracing can often be omitted. Decide whether trim is to be applied on top of the siding or butted into it. If butted, apply trim first, then apply siding. Horizontal wood siding is more expensive than plywood panel siding but provides an attractive and durable exterior. However, horizontal wood siding requires periodic painting for preservation.

Figure 43A - Siding Alternatives

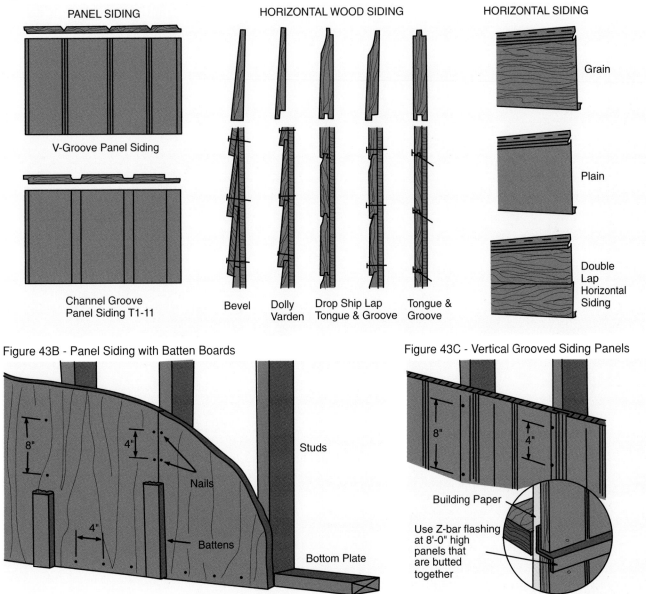

PANEL SIDING

V-Groove Panel Siding

Channel Groove Panel Siding T1-11

HORIZONTAL WOOD SIDING

Bevel

Dolly Varden

Drop Ship Lap Tongue & Groove

Tongue & Groove

HORIZONTAL SIDING

Grain

Plain

Double Lap Horizontal Siding

Figure 43B - Panel Siding with Batten Boards

8"

4"

4"

Nails

Battens

Studs

Bottom Plate

Figure 43C - Vertical Grooved Siding Panels

8"

4"

Building Paper

Use Z-bar flashing at 8'-0" high panels that are butted together

Siding

Horizontal Siding

Lay down various lengths of siding at each side. Apply so that joints in the succeeding course do not fall directly above each other. Butt all joints over the center of a stud. Seal by painting the edges with primer before butting. Start the bottom of the first course 1/2" below the bottom plate. Siding on all walls should be aligned and level and each course equally spaced. Be especially careful to determine the lap and exposure to the weather before applying the second and succeeding courses. Measure the distance to be covered and divide it by the desired exposure to get the total number of courses of siding. See Figure 44B below. Carefully mark these spaces on the corners of each wall, taking into consideration the overlap of the siding. Run a chalk line from one mark to another, leaving a horizontal chalk line on the building paper as a guide. If you are not applying sheathing or building paper, chalk the wall studs directly. Apply the siding and keep it consistent by checking with your level.

Final openings, where siding meets the soffit if applicable, can be closed with a piece of quarter round or shingle mould. Protect your garage by painting or staining it as soon as possible.

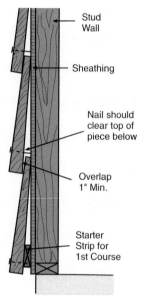

Figure 44A - Horizontal Siding Detail

- Stud Wall
- Sheathing
- Nail should clear top of piece below
- Overlap 1" Min.
- Starter Strip for 1st Course

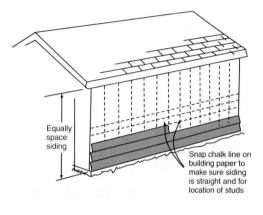

Figure 44B - Marking Siding Courses

Equally space siding

Snap chalk line on building paper to make sure siding is straight and for location of studs

Vinyl Siding

Vinyl siding must be installed over a smooth surface such as wood or foam sheathing. If you are using drip-in foam backer or contoured backer make sure it meets your vinyl manufacturer's specifications. When installing vinyl siding it is recommended you use galvanized nails with smooth shank and flat heads. Remember to place nails in the center of the slot and do not nail tightly. If panels are not spaced properly allowing for expansion or nailed properly they may buckle in hot weather. No matter if you are installing siding horizontally or vertically all corner trim, window and door trim along with starter strips are installed first. Take extra care when installing the starter strip insuring that it is level. Next you should install the trim for under the soffits and gable rakes. Now you are ready to install the siding panels. Snap the first panel into the starter strip and continue up the wall. Make sure to stagger joints and overlap siding ends 1" but cut nailing flange back 1-1/2" to allow for expansion. After installation is complete, caulk seams that water may penetrate but do not caulk between panel ends or trim strips. It is recommended you read the manufacturer's installation guide before starting the installation process.

Building Paper

Some local building codes might require that building paper be used to seal the wall from the elements. Building paper is typically felt or kraft paper impregnated with asphalt and is stapled or nailed between the siding and the sheathing or studs. Rolls are usually 36" wide and come in lengths covering between 200 to 500 square feet. Apply building paper in horizontal strips from the bottom of the wall as shown in Figure 44C. Overlaps should be 2" at horizontal joints, 6" at vertical joints, and 12" at corners. Cutting is done with a utility knife. Use just enough staples or nails to hold the paper in place. Siding nails will hold it permanently. Before you install siding, snap a level chalk line on the siding to indicate the bottom edge of the paper and work up.

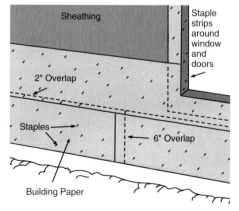

Figure 44C - Applying Building Paper

- Sheathing
- Staple strips around window and doors
- 2" Overlap
- Staples
- 6" Overlap
- Building Paper

Garage Doors

One of the most important aspects of building a garage is selecting the door. Due to the size of lots, building restrictions, and other reasons, the garage often takes an up-front position in visibility, in many cases the garage door is more prominent than the front door of the home. You will want a door that is compatible and attractive as well as utilitarian. There is a large selection of styles and patterns from which to choose in today's market.

Governing factors are usually visual appeal and budget. The door can be as plain or as ornate as you wish. It can be made of wood, fiberglass, aluminum, or steel, and it can even be insulated with a poly core. It should be solid, constructed of materials that will stand a fair amount of hard use, and it should be lightweight and balanced so that even the children in the family can operate it.

But most important are the headroom requirements and the doorjamb. If the jamb is improperly constructed, you will have nothing but grief with any door, no matter what type or quality. So, carefully check the specifications of the door manufacturer you select.

Figure 45 - Typical Garage Door Designs

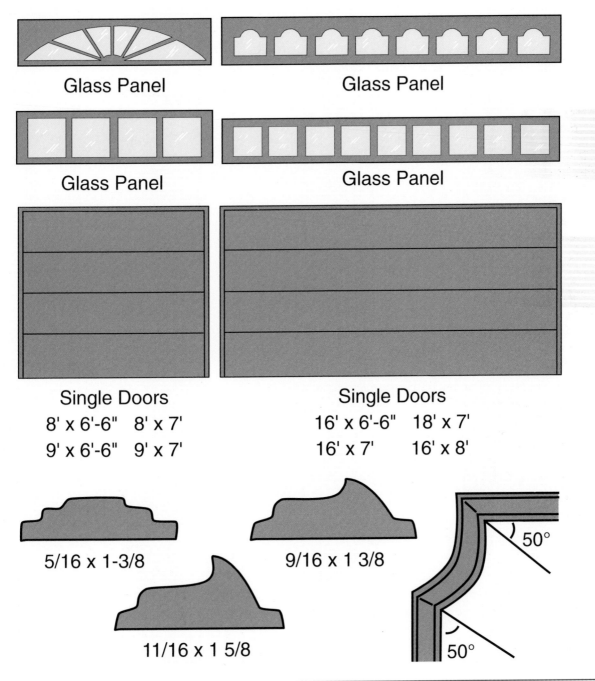

Glass Panel

Glass Panel

Glass Panel

Glass Panel

Single Doors
8' x 6'-6"   8' x 7'
9' x 6'-6"   9' x 7'

Single Doors
16' x 6'-6"   18' x 7'
16' x 7'   16' x 8'

5/16 x 1-3/8

9/16 x 1 3/8

11/16 x 1 5/8

50°

50°

Door Mouldings

Moulding patterns and layout designs are almost as varied for garage doors as they are for the door to your house and are a great way to brighten up the front of your garage. The patterns shown here are just a suggestion of the many styles there are to choose from. Choose one or a combination of patterns, but keep in mind that the style size of your door might affect the choice of moulding. What works on an upward-working solid door might not work as well or look as good on a sectional or a side-acting door.

Remember that accurate measurements are important for mitering, especially since all the pieces should be cut to size before you are ready to attach them to the door. Also remember that the doors will be exposed to varied weather conditions, so they will need to be sealed, stained, or painted accordingly.

Figure 46 - Typical Garage Door Mouldings

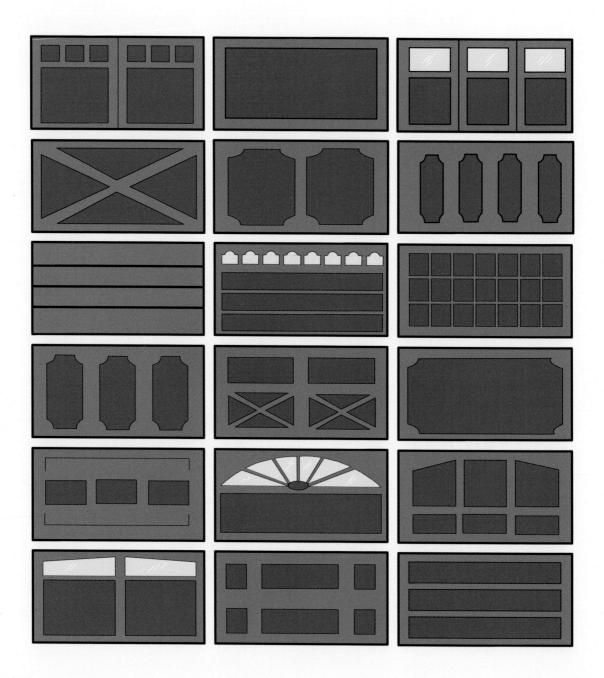

Sectional Garage Doors

Sectional garage doors are comprised of several horizontal sections held together with hinges. The side hinges have rollers so that the door section can roll up or down as a single unit. Rollers, track, and brackets are made to fit the sides and top of the door against the door frame for a snug weather-tight seal. The bottom of the door should be weatherstripped. Standard rubber gasket stripping provides an especially tight fit.

Installation instructions for the door and its hardware are provided by the door manufacturer, but it is strongly recommended that this work be done by a professional. The torsion springs used to help lift and balance most door designs store tremendous amounts of energy and can cause severe bodily injury and or property damage if accidentally released during installation or operation.

Hardware Details

The torsion spring-type sectional door is operated by an assembly consisting of one or more torsion springs, a continuous torsion shaft, two lift drums, two lift cables, and associated hardware, including drum, torsion, shaft, torsion spring bearing, and bearing brackets. Track, roller bearings, and all hardware should be kept clean and lubricated. But as mentioned previously, all installation and adjustment of the system must be done by a professional.

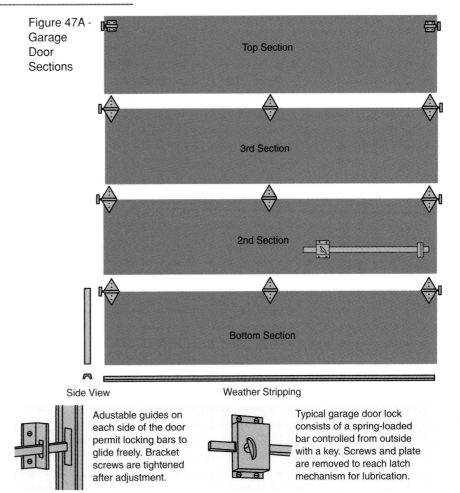

Figure 47A - Garage Door Sections

Top Section

3rd Section

2nd Section

Bottom Section

Side View

Weather Stripping

Adustable guides on each side of the door permit locking bars to glide freely. Bracket screws are tightened after adjustment.

Typical garage door lock consists of a spring-loaded bar controlled from outside with a key. Screws and plate are removed to reach latch mechanism for lubrication.

Figure 47B - Garage door with single spring across door opening. This spring winds instead of stretching. Tension is adjusted by loosening the collar locknut and winding it tighter with a bar inserted through the collar.

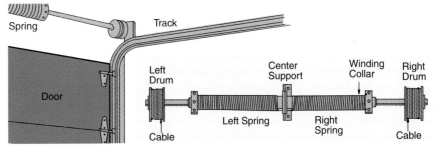

Spring   Track

Door

Left Drum   Center Support   Winding Collar   Right Drum

Left Spring   Right Spring

Cable   Cable

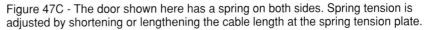

Figure 47C - The door shown here has a spring on both sides. Spring tension is adjusted by shortening or lengthening the cable length at the spring tension plate.

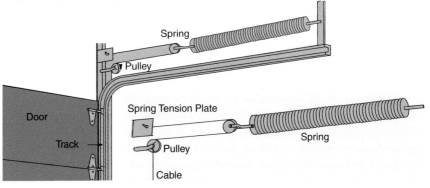

Spring

Pulley

Door

Track

Spring Tension Plate

Spring

Pulley

Cable

Installing Prehung Doors

Prehung doors are assembled at the factory. The door comes hinged and mounted on the side jamb with a hole drilled through the door for the doorknob. A right-hand door or left-hand door is determined by the side of the door on which the knob is located, viewed from inside the room into which it opens.

The door is installed by placing it into the rough opening and shimming it to make it square. Don't count on the opening being square.

After you've shimmed it so that the jamb is centered in the door opening, hold it in place by driving a 12d casing nail through the shims and into the trimmer stud near the top of the hinge-side jamb. Nail the head jamb to the header after making sure everything is square.

Again make sure the frame is centered and square, then secure the hinge side by nailing into the trimmer stud through the shims. Check that the door swings freely, then secure the other jamb. Weatherstripping is built into the threshold. The door must be removed to screw it to the existing threshold, and then measure and cut door to fit.

Figure 48 - Fitting Doors

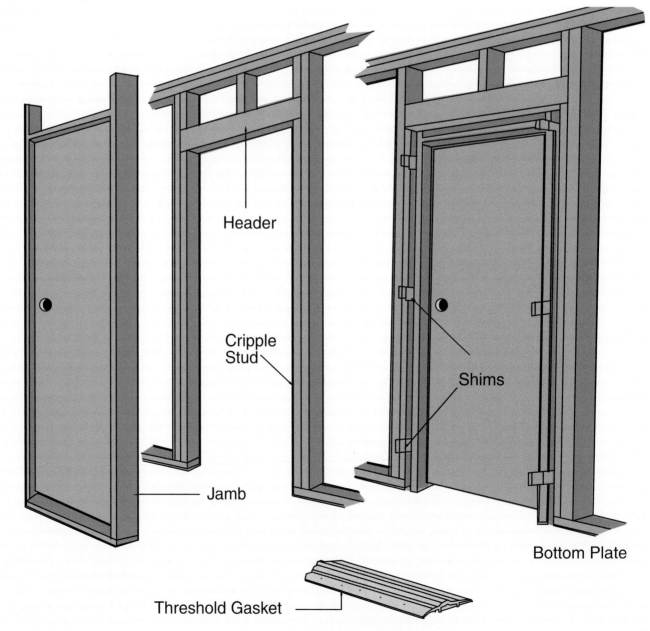

Header

Cripple Stud

Shims

Jamb

Bottom Plate

Threshold Gasket

Disappearing Stairs

Folding stairways are factory-assembled for installation as a unit. The jamb is nailed to joists, and springs act as a counterbalance to the stairway and ceiling panel for easy operation. They are well suited to areas with limited head space, such as a garage loft, because the jambs and folded ladder use very little vertical space above the ceiling. Stair treads are normally painted with nonskid paint. Manufacturers provide installation instructions.

Disappearing Stair Sizes

Rough Opening	Floor To Ceiling	Ladder Width
22" x 48"	7'-10" to 8'-5"	14"
22" x 54"	8'-6" to 10'-0"	14"
30" x 60"	7'-10" to 8'-9"	22"
30" x 60"	8'-10" to 10'-0"	22"

Figure 49 - Folding Stairways

Building the Stairway

A stair assembly consists of stringers, risers, treads, and often railings. To build your stairs, begin by laying out the cut marks on the 2x12s to be used for stringers. Use a carpenter's square with the tread dimensions marked on the body of the square and the riser dimensions on the square tongue. Cuts can be made with either a handsaw or a circular saw, but final cuts should be hand-made.

Remember that the bottom edge of the riser rests on the tread beneath it, while the forward edge of the tread is flush or overhangs the riser beneath it. A 1-1/8" overhang creates a professional look.

Cut out one stringer first and check its alignment. If it is correct, use it as a master for the second stringer. A third one will also need to be cut if the stairs are 36" wide or more.

Nail the top of the stringer to trimmers or header of the rough opening. For additional strength, an extra header board, a ledger, or joist hangers can be used. The bottoms are toenailed to the floor or to a 2x4 bottom ledger.

Attach treads first with 12d nails, then nail on the riser with 8d nails. Gluing the risers and treads to the stringers, along with nailing, will help reduce noise. Check local building codes for stair construction.

Figure 50A - Laying Out a Stringer

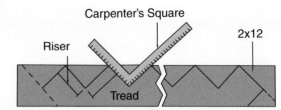

Figure 50B - Typical Stairway

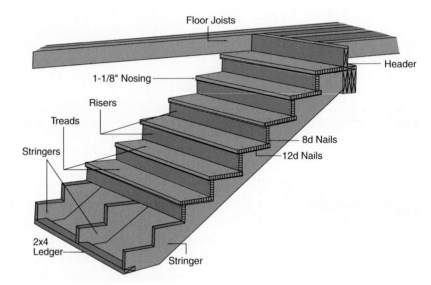

Figure 50C - Typical Stair Detail

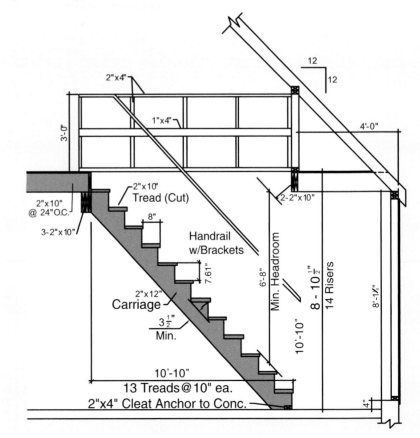

Electrical Wiring

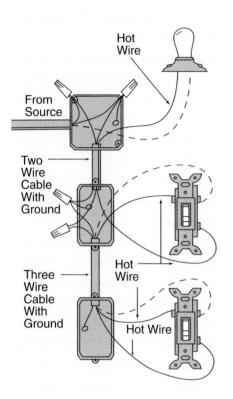

If you plan on wiring your garage for electricity and are considering doing it yourself, two stops are almost mandatory: your local building code office and the power company, in that order. The code office will be able to inform you of any local wiring requirements, and they can be quite specific. They can also vary widely from one area to another. Don't bet on the code being exactly the same as it was in the last town you lived. Even though many municipalities use the National Electrical Code (NEC), which spells out uniform safety standards for wiring methods and materials, it is often modified from one municipality to another to meet local needs. Checking with the code office can advise you of those variations, as well as setting you up on permit inspection requirements. It will also advise you whether or not there are any requirements for using a professional electrician during the wiring. Remember that whether or not there are such requirements, if there's something that you're not sure of when you are putting in the wiring, it's best to have professional assistance.

The power company will be able to tell you the best or required location for a meter and service panel if the garage will be separately serviced. If you plan on running off existing home service, you can avoid trouble by making sure that the existing lines are able to carry the additional load.

Layout the location of all outlet boxes and lights on a floor plan of the garage to help in estimating material requirements. Plan on several outlets if you will use the garage as a workshop area, and be sure there is plenty of lighting for safety purposes. It is best to plan now to avoid headaches later. If you are installing an overhead garage door opener, you will also need a three-prong ceiling outlet placed in the proper position.

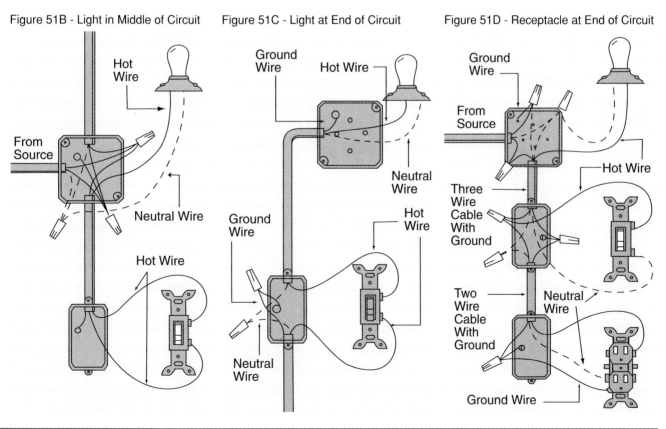

Figure 51B - Light in Middle of Circuit

Figure 51C - Light at End of Circuit

Figure 51D - Receptacle at End of Circuit

Garage Door Opener

One of the most common garage accessories is the automatic garage door opener. It is available in a wide range of models from a number of manufacturers, generally at moderate expense and with a variety of features. Besides permitting you to open the garage door in stormy weather or at night without leaving your car, openers can provide interior garage lighting and a secure locking system.

Unlike the actual door and hardware, the opener itself is something you can easily install yourself. Carefully follow the manufacturer's instructions for mounting the opener at the correct height and securing it to the door header and the door.

Most openers offer a programmable remote control transmitter so you can personally select the radio frequency that opens your door. A separate wall-mounted switch is also a convenient feature to look for when selecting your opener.

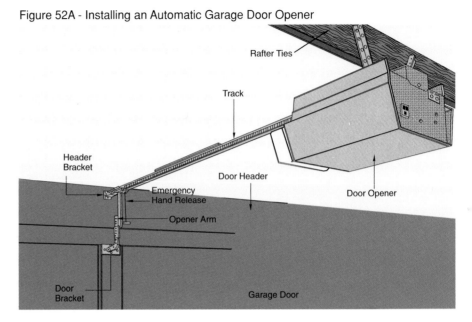

Figure 52A - Installing an Automatic Garage Door Opener

Garage Storage Ideas

A. Quick and easy storage can be found for items that don't need to be readily accessible by keeping them on boards or plywood sheets laid perpendicular to the joists.

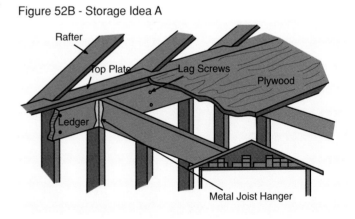

Figure 52B - Storage Idea A

Figure 52C - Storage Idea B

B. Hanging cabinets keep articles used often at hand. Use an eyehook to hold drop doors out of the way when the cabinet is being used.

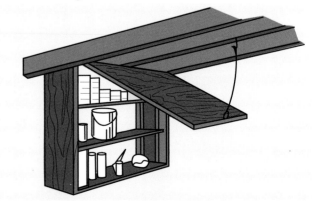

Garage Storage Ideas

Figure 53A - Storage Idea C

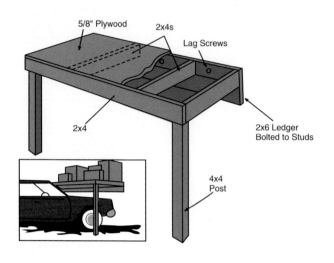

C. For storage of bulk goods, construction of an over-the-hood platform is an easy and worthwhile task.

D. Garages quickly become catch-alls. Hanging cabinets will give you additional storage space for less bulky items without taking up valuable floor space.

Figure 53B - Storage Idea D

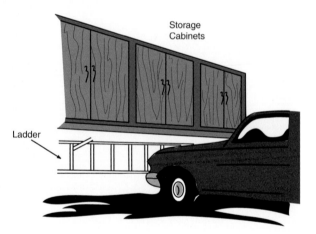

E. Smaller items can be stored on projecting shelves hung on studs or closed walls.

F. Overhanging brackets are easy to make and offer out-of-the way storage for items such as lumber, pipes, etc.
Note: Additional reinforcing of ceiling joists may be required to accommodate overhanging storage.

Figure 53C - Storage Idea E

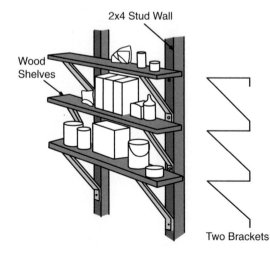

Figure 53D - Storage Idea F

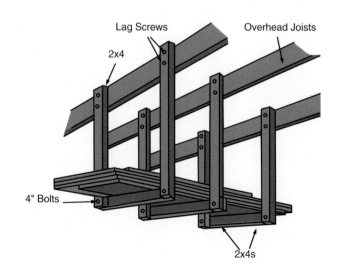

Garage Storage Ideas

Figure 54A - Storage Idea G

1x12

2x4

1x2

G. If you've got the space, deep shelves can be built quickly and simply with furring strips (1x2s), 2x4s, and plywood or 1x12s.

H. Be creative. One of a garage's big advantages is that there are very few set storage rules. A set-up like this is made out of 2x4s and plywood gets not only the bikes out of the way, but other items as well.

Figure 54B - Storage Idea H

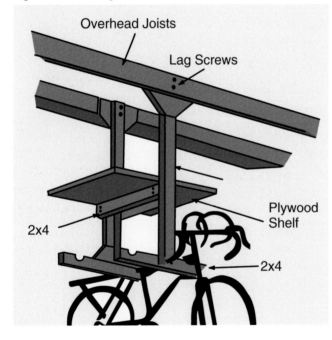

Overhead Joists

Lag Screws

Plywood Shelf

2x4

2x4

I. Where space is tight, a couple of blocks nailed to the studs serve as good shelf supports. All you need is some 1x4s and you can build all the small-item storage you want.

J. Screw jar lids to the bottoms of shelves, and the jars become conveniently stored, portable clutter containers.

Figure 54C - Storage Idea I

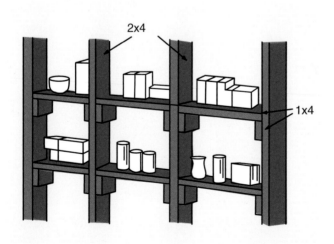

2x4

1x4

Figure 54D - Storage Idea J

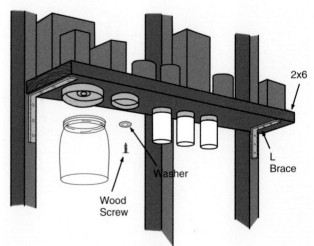

2x6

Washer

Wood Screw

L Brace

Garage Storage Ideas

Figure 55A - Storage Idea K

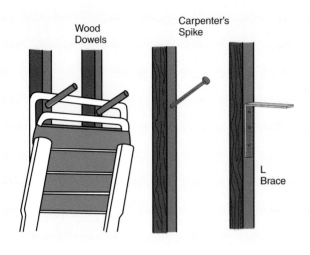

Wood Dowels

Carpenter's Spike

L Brace

K. Spikes, dowels, or wall brackets make great hangers on studs for many light items.

L. Pegboards and spring clips keep things visible, handy, and produce a tidy, organized effect.

M. Small storage compartments made of plywood or similar material can be hung from the ceiling joists to keep seasonal items organized and clean.
Note: Additional reinforcing of ceiling joists may be required to accommodate storage compartments.

Figure 55B - Storage Idea L

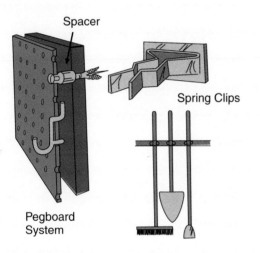

Spacer

Spring Clips

Pegboard System

N. You've got to put a ladder somewhere. The garage is long enough, so hang it from the ceiling rather than leaving it on the floor where somebody is bound to trip over it or knock it down.

Figure 55C - Storage Idea M

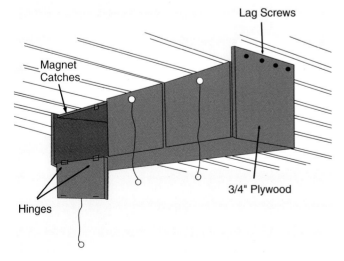

Lag Screws

Magnet Catches

Hinges

3/4" Plywood

Figure 55D - Storage Idea N

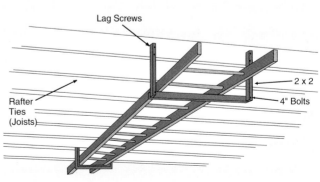

Lag Screws

Rafter Ties (Joists)

2 x 2

4" Bolts

Finishing the Inside of Your Garage

You can either finish the interior of your garage with drywall or leave the wall studs exposed and use blocking to build shelving between the studs. Some garage builders will want to take advantage of the extra storage space afforded by the open wall sections. Use your imagination to create additional storage space by nailing or screwing 1x2 cleats to the studs and then installing extended horizontal shelving over the cleats.

If you elect to install 4'x8' drywall panels (also known as wallboard) in your garage, study the illustrations below for suggestions on nailing or gluing drywall to wall studs. There are many different thicknesses available for drywall panel installation. Although 1/2" drywall is common, 5/8" drywall is being required for most residential municipalities. Check with your local building department before drywall installation.

A variety of fasteners are available for wallboard. Consult your local home center or building material supplier for suggestions. After you have installed the panels, you can tape and fill the joints with joint compound or simply cover the joints with tape if the final appearance is not a major concern.

Figure 56A - Nailing Wallboard

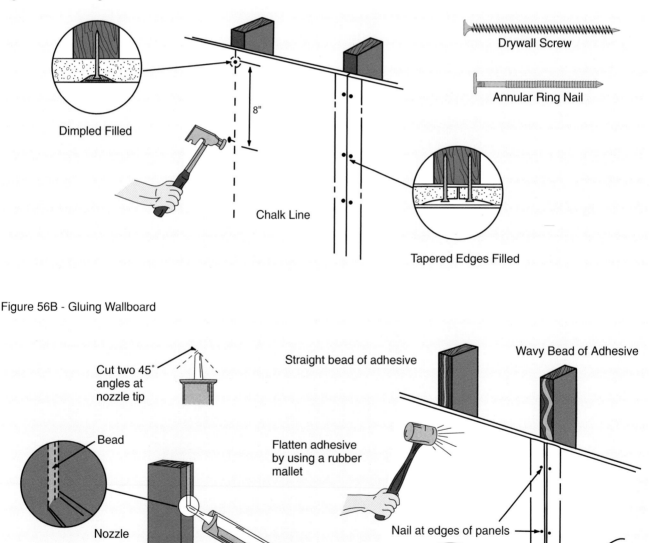

Figure 56B - Gluing Wallboard

For Notes and Layout Procedures

For Notes and Layout Procedures

Scale: ½" = 1'-0" per square

For Notes and Layout Procedures

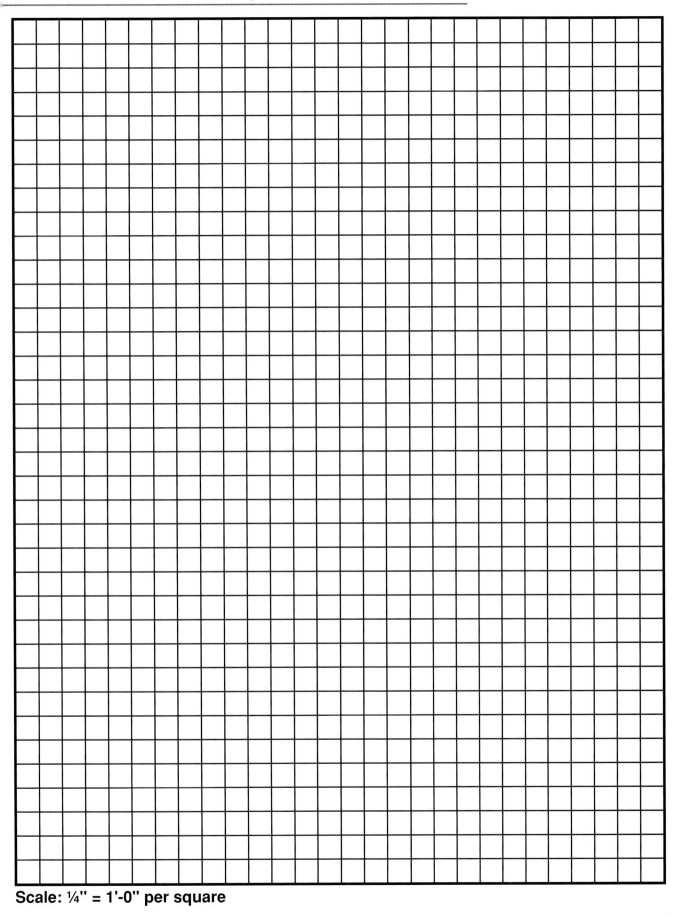

Scale: ¼" = 1'-0" per square

Glossary

Anchor Bolt - A metal connector device used to connect a wood mudsill to a concrete wall or slab.

Batterboards - Scrap lumber nailed horizontally to stakes driven near each corner of the foundation excavation. Stretch nylon strings between batterboards to transfer reference points and to measure elevation.

Beam - Beams are horizontal structural members that are supported by vertical posts. Beams are typically constructed from 2 or more 2xs, 4x material, or engineered lumber.

Bottom Plate - In stud wall framing, the bottom horizontal member of the wall. Also known as the soleplate.

Bridging - Wood or metal cross pieces fastened between floor joists to provide structural strength.

Cantilever - Refers to the end portion of a joist that extends beyond the beam.

Casing - Molding around door and window openings.

Codes - Regulations implemented by your local building department which control the design and construction of buildings and other structures. Consult your local building department for applicable codes before you begin your construction project.

Collar Beam - A connecting member used between rafters to strengthen the roof structure.

Cornice - The structure created at the eave overhang which typically consists of fascia board, soffit, and moldings.

Cripple Studs - Short studs that strengthen window and door openings or the gable end of a roof. Also known as jack studs.

Darby - A flat tool with two handles used for spreading concrete, plaster or stucco.

Defect - Any defect in lumber whether a result of a manufacturing imperfection or an irregularity in the timber from which the lumber was cut. Some defects are only blemishes while others can reduce strength and durability. Grading rules establish the extent and severity of wood defects.

Drip Edge - Angled metal or wood located on the outer edge of the roof. Drip edge prevents water penetration.

Drywall - A gypsum panel used to finish interior walls. Also known as plasterboard or sheet rock.

Eave - The roof overhang projecting beyond the exterior wall.

Edge - The narrowest side of a piece of lumber that is perpendicular to both the face and the end.

Elevation - Drawing of a structure as it will appear from the front, rear, left and right sides.

Engineered Lumber - Refers to beams or rafters constructed from wood fiber and glue such as glu-lams, micro-lams, or wood I-beams. Often superior in strength and durability to dimensional lumber.

Face - The widest side of a piece of lumber that is perpendicular to both the edge and the end.

Fascia - Trim used along the eave or gable end.

Finish - Any protective coating applied to your structure to protect against weathering. Finishes are available as stains, paints, or preservatives.

Flakeboard - A panel material made from compressed wood chips bonded with resin. Also known as oriented strand board (OSB) or chipboard.

Flashing - Metal material used on the roof and eaves to prevent moisture penetration.

Fly Rafters - Rafters at the gable end that "fly" unsupported by the tie plate. Also known as rack, barge, or verge rafters.

Footing - Concrete footings help to anchor your foundation or piers in the surrounding soil and distribute weight over a larger surface area. In climates where the soil freezes, a generous footing protects against soil heaves and structural slippage.

Frieze - A horizontal framing member that connects the siding with the soffit.

Frost Line - Measure of the maximum penetration of frost in the soil in a given geographic location. Depth of frost penetration varies with climate conditions.

Furring - Narrow strips of wood attached to walls or other surfaces that serve as a fastening base for drywall.

Gable - The triangular end of the roof structure formed by the roof framing.

Galvanized Nails - Hot-dipped galvanized nails (HDG) are dipped in zinc and will not rust.

Girder - Same as beam.

Grade Stamp - A stamp imprinted on dimensional lumber that identifies wood species, grade, texture, moisture content, and usage. Grade descriptions such as select, finish, and common signify limiting characteristics that may occur in lumber in each grade. The stamp indicates a uniform measurement of performance that permits lumber of a given grade to be used for the same purpose, regardless of the manufacturer.

Grading - The process of excavating, leveling, and compacting the soil or gravel beneath your foundation to its desired finish level. Proper grading avoids drainage problems.

Grain - Lumber shows either a flat or vertical grain depending on how it was cut from the log. To minimize warping along the face of lumber (known as cupping) and raising of the grain, you should place flat grain lumber with the bark side up or facing out.

Header - A horizontal load-bearing support member over an opening in the wall such as window or door openings.

Heartwood - Core of the log that resists decay.

Hip Rafter - A short rafter that forms the hip of a roof and runs from the corner of a wall to the ridge board. Usually set at a 45-degree angle to the walls.

Jack Rafter - A short rafter that runs from the ridge board to a hip or valley rafter or from the hip rafter to the tie plate.

Joist - Lumber that is set on edge and supports a floor, decking, or ceiling. Joists in turn are supported by beams and posts.

Joist Hanger - A metal connector available in many sizes and styles that attaches to a ledge or rim joist and makes a secure butt joint between ledger and joist.

Lag Screw - Heavy-duty fastener with hexagonal bolt head that provides extra fastening power for critical structural connections. Use galvanized lag screws to prevent rust.

Glossary

Ledger - A horizontal support member to which joists or other support members are attached.

Let-in Brace - Usually a 1x4 corner brace in a wall section that runs diagonally from the bottom to top plate.

Look-out - Blocking which extends from an inner common rafter to the fly rafters at the gable ends.

Metal Connectors - Used to augment or replace nails as fasteners, metal connectors are critical for lasting and sturdy garage construction.

Moisture Content - Moisture content of wood is the weight of water in wood expressed as a percentage of the weight of wood from which all water has been removed. The drier the lumber the less the lumber will shrink and warp. Surfaced lumber with a moisture content of 19% or less is known as dry lumber and is typically grade stamped as "S-DRY." Moisture content over 19% results in a "S-GRN" stamp to indicate surfaced green.

Mudsill - The part of the wall framing that contacts the foundation. It should be pressure-treated to resist moisture and decay. Also known as the sill plate.

Outrigger - An extension of a rafter at the eave used to form a cornice or overhang on a roof.

Pea Gravel - Approximately 1/4" round gravel material used in a 4"-6" layer to cover the soil under your concrete slab.

Perpendicular - At a 90 degree or right angle.

Pilot Hole - A slightly undersized hole drilled in lumber that prevents splitting of the wood when nailed.

Pitch - A measurement of roof slope. Expressed as the ratio of the total rise divided by the span.

Plumb - Absolutely vertical. Determined with either a plumb bob or spirit level.

Post - A vertical support member that bears the weight of the joists and beams. Typically posts are at least 4x4 lumber.

Pressure-Treated - Refers to the process of forcing preservative compounds into the fiber of the wood. Handle pressure-treated lumber with caution and do not inhale or burn its sawdust. Certain types of pressure-treated lumber are suitable for ground contact use while others must be used above ground. While more expensive than untreated lumber, pressure-treated wood resists decay and is recommended where naturally decay-resistant species like cedar or redwood are unavailable or too costly.

Purlin - A horizontal member of the roof framing that supports rafters or spans between trusses.

Rafter - A roof framing member that extends from the top plate to the ridge board and supports the roof sheathing and roofing material.

Rake - The inclined end area of a gable roof.

Redwood - Decay-resistant and stable wood for exterior use. Heartwood grades provide the greatest decay resistance.

Reinforcing Bar - A steel rod that provides internal reinforcement for concrete piers and foundations. Also known as rebar.

Ridge Board - A 1x or typically 2x member on edge at the roof's peak to which the rafters are connected.

Right Triangle, 6-8-10 or 3-4-5 - A means of insuring squareness when you lay out your foundations. Mark a vertical line at exactly 8'-0" from the angle you want to square. Then mark a horizontal line at exactly 6'-0" from the crossing vertical line. Measure the distance diagonally between both the 6'-0" and 8'-0" marks and when the distance measures 10'-0" exactly you have squared a 90 degree angle between lines.

Rise - In roof construction the vertical distance the ridge rises above the top plate at the center of the span.

Rough Sill - The lowest framing member of a door or window opening.

Scale - A system of representation in plan drawing where small dimensions represent an equivalent large dimension. Most construction plans are said to be scaled down. Scale is expressed as an equation such as 1/4"=1-0'.

Screed - A straight piece of lumber used to level wet concrete or the gravel.

Sheathing - Exterior sheet (typically 4' x 8') material fastened to the rafter or exterior stud walls.

Slope - A measurement of inclination and is expressed as a percentage of units of vertical rise per units of horizontal distance.

Soffit - The underside of the roof overhang. Soffits can either be closed or open (thus exposing the roof rafters).

Span - The distance between two opposing walls as measured from the outside of the top plates or the distance between two beam supports that are measured from center to center.

Spirit Level - A sealed cylinder with a transparent tube nearly filled with liquid forming a bubble used to indicate true vertical and horizontal alignment when the bubble is centered in the length of the tube.

String Level - A spirit level mounted in a frame with prongs at either end for hanging on a string. Determines level across string lines.

Stud - The vertical framing member of a wall.

T1-11 Siding - Exterior siding material with vertical grooves usually 8" on center.

Tie Plate - The framing member nailed to the top plates in order to connect and align wall sections. Also known as the cap plate or second top plate.

Toenail - To drive a nail at an angle. When you toenail a post to a beam for example, drive the nail so that one-half the nail is in each member.

Top Plate - The horizontal top part of the wall framing perpendicular to the wall studs.

Tongue and Groove - Refers to the milling of lumber so that adjacent parts interlock for added strength and durability.

Trimmer Stud - The stud adjacent to window or door opening studs which strengthens the opening and bears the weight of the window or door headers. Also known as a jack stud.

Truss - A triangular prefabricated unit for supporting a roof load over a span. Trusses are relatively lightweight and can offer an easier method of roof construction for the novice.

Valley Rafter - A rafter running from a tie plate at the corner of a wall along the roof valley and up to the ridge.

Ready to Start Some Serious Planning?

Now that you have read this do-it-yourself manual, you're ready to start serious planning. As you can see, there are many details to consider, and they all tie together for successful completion of your garage project.

If the procedures appear at first confusing, reread the information outlined in this book several times before deciding which phases of construction you want to handle yourself and which might require professional assistance.

Because drawing up your own plan from scratch can be time consuming and difficult for the inexperienced builder, you might want to make planning and cost estimating easier by selecting a design from those shown in this book.

If blueprints with lumber lists are not immediately available from your building material dealer, you can order them by using the order form in the back of this book. If after reviewing the blueprints you still have questions, talk them over with your lumber dealer. Most dealers are familiar with construction and will be glad to help you.

The following pages include an assortment of garage plans and other projects. Remember that construction blueprints can be obtained from your dealer or by using the order form on page 160. All blueprint plans include a complete material list, exterior elevations, sections, details and instructions for the successful completion of your project.

Example of a Typical Project Plan Sheet

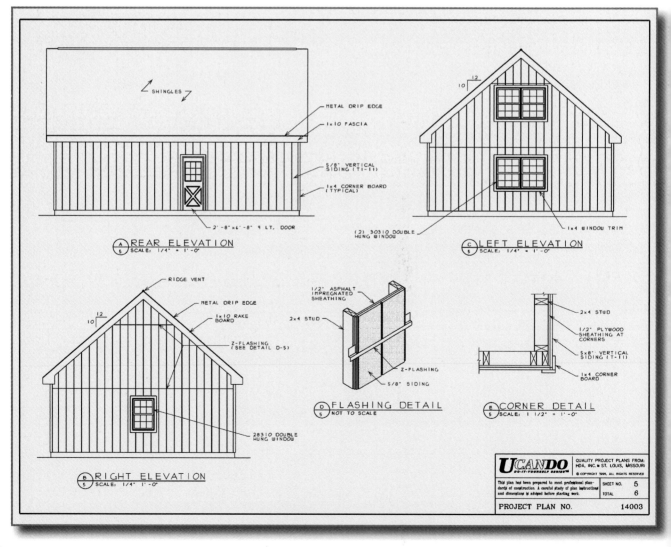

Project Plans
Garages, Workshops, and MORE

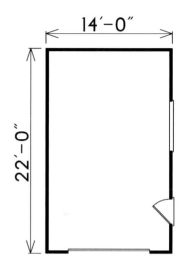

Plan #GM3-002D-6005

Price Code P8

14'-0"

22'-0"

1-Car Garage

- Size - 14' x 22'
- Building height - 10'-10"
- Roof pitch - 4/12
- Ceiling height - 8'
- 9' x 7' overhead door
- Side window enhances exterior
- Side entry is convenient
- Complete list of materials
- Step-by-step instructions

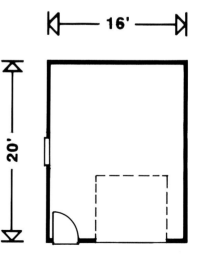

Plan #GM3-063D-6011

Price Code P8

16'

20'

1-Car Garage with Front Door

- Size - 16' x 20'
- Building height - 13'
- Roof pitch - 5/12
- Ceiling height - 8'
- 9' x 7' overhead door
- Complete list of materials

Plan #GM3-002D-6022

Price Code P8

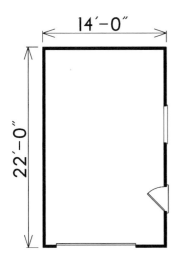

14'-0"

22'-0"

1-Car Garage - Western Style

- Size - 14' x 22'
- Building height - 10'-10"
- Roof pitch - 4/12
- Ceiling height - 8'
- 9' x 7' overhead door
- Compact size is perfect for smaller lots
- Efficient side door provides easy access
- Complete list of materials
- Step-by-step instructions

Plan #GM3-059D-6009

Price Code P8

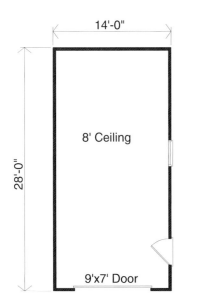

14'-0"

8' Ceiling

28'-0"

9'x7' Door

1-Car Garage with Depth

- Size - 14' x 28'
- Building height - 13'
- Roof pitch - 6/12
- Ceiling height - 8'
- 9' x 7' overhead door
- Side door allows for easy access
- Complete list of materials

1-Car Garage with Loft

- Size - 16' x 24'
- Building height - 18'-9"
- Roof pitch - 6/12, 12/6
- Ceiling height - 8'
- Loft ceiling height - 6'-7"
- 9' x 7' overhead door
- Ideal loft perfect for workshop or storage area
- Handy side door
- Complete list of materials
- Step-by-step instructions

Plan #GM3-002D-6043

Price Code P9

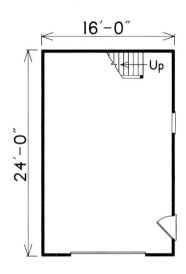

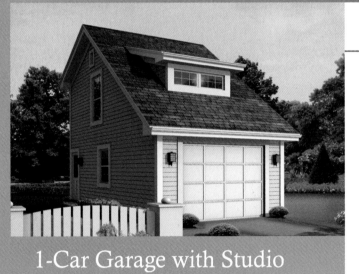

1-Car Garage with Studio

- Size - 14' x 26'
- Building height - 22'
- Roof pitch - 6/12, 10/12
- Ceiling heights -
    First floor - 8'   Second floor - 8'
- 9' x 7' overhead door
- Garage features a bonus storage area below the stairs and access door to the second floor
- The second floor includes an open studio room
- Complete list of materials

Plan #GM3-009D-6013

Price Code P10

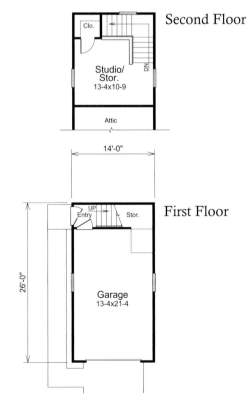

Second Floor

First Floor

Plan #GM3-002D-6010

Price Code P9

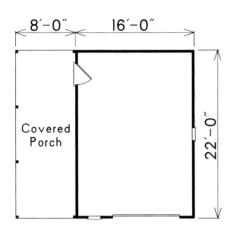

1-Car Garage with Covered Porch

- Size - 24' x 22'
- Building height - 13'
- Roof pitch - 5/12
- Ceiling height - 8'
- 9' x 7' overhead door
- Distinctive covered porch provides area for entertaining
- Complete list of materials
- Step-by-step instructions

Plan #GM3-002D-6028

Price Code P8

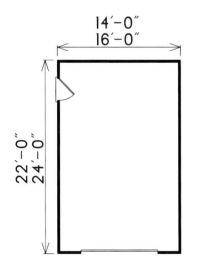

1-Car Garages

- Four popular sizes -
   14' x 22'   14' x 24'
   16' x 22'   16' x 24'
- Building height - 11'-2"
- Roof pitch - 4/12
- Ceiling height - 8'
- 9' x 7' overhead door
- Sturdy, attractive design
- Complete list of materials
- Step-by-step instructions

To order online visit www.projectplans.com

Plan #GM3-002D-6045

Price Code P9

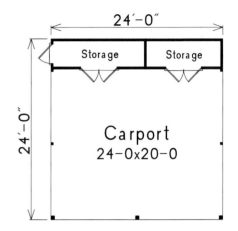

2-Car Carport with Storage

- Size - 24' x 24'
- Building height - 12'-8"
- Roof pitch - 4/12
- Ceiling height - 8'
- Unique design allows cars to enter from the front or side of the carport
- Deep storage space for long or tall items
- Complete list of materials
- Step-by-step instructions

Plan #GM3-059D-6020

Price Code P8

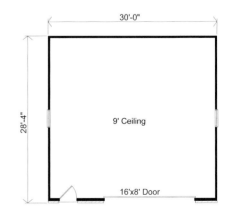

2-Car Garage with Front Door

- Size - 30'-0" x 28'-4"
- Building height - 18'
- Roof pitch - 6/12, 7/12
- Ceiling height - 9'
- Convenient front door provides easy access
- Brick veneer adds elegance to this garage plan
- Complete list of materials

Plan #GM3-002D-6030

Price Code P10

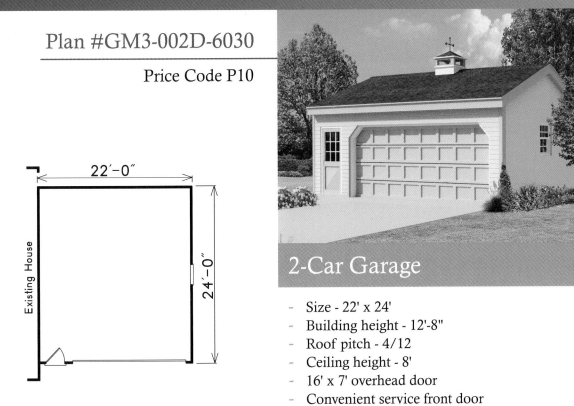

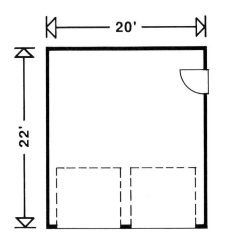

22'-0"

24'-0"

Existing House

2-Car Garage

- Size - 22' x 24'
- Building height - 12'-8"
- Roof pitch - 4/12
- Ceiling height - 8'
- 16' x 7' overhead door
- Convenient service front door
- Traditionally styled
- Complete list of materials
- Step-by-step instructions

Plan #GM3-063D-6013

Price Code P8

20'

22'

Front Gable 2-Car Garage

- Size - 20' x 22'
- Building height - 12'-6"
- Roof pitch - 5/12
- Ceiling height - 8'
- Two 9' x 7' overhead doors
- Side entry door for easy access
- Complete list of materials

Compact 2-Car Garage

- Size - 20' x 20'
- Building height - 14'
- Roof pitch - 5/12
- Ceiling height - 8'
- 16' x 7' overhead door
- Excellent small garage for many different home styles
- Complete list of materials

Plan #GM3-059D-6021

Price Code P8

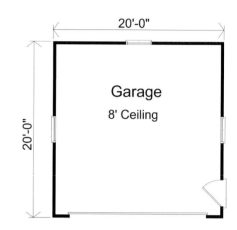

Plan #GM3-063D-6002

Price Code P9

2-Car Garage with Loft

- Size - 32' x 26'
- Building height - 23'
- Roof pitch - 12/12
- Ceiling heights -
    First floor - 8'   Second floor - 8'
- Two 9' x 7' overhead doors
- Handy workbench with plenty of workspace
- Additional storage available in loft
- Complete list of materials

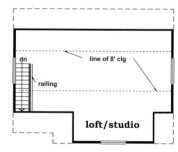

Second Floor

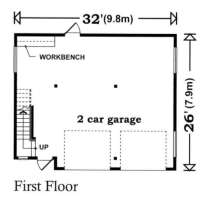

First Floor

Plan #GM3-002D-6031

Price Code P10

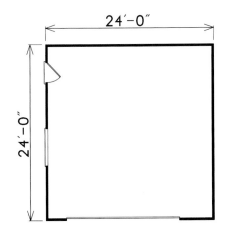

24'-0"

24'-0"

2-Car Garage - Gambrel Roof

- Size - 24' x 24'
- Building height - 15'-5"
- Roof pitch - 4/12, 12/8
- Ceiling height - 8'
- 16' x 7' overhead door
- Attractive addition to any home
- Complete list of materials
- Step-by-step instructions

Plan #GM3-009D-6017

Price Code P10

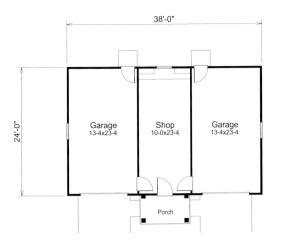

38'-0"

24'-0"

Garage
13-4x23-4

Shop
10-0x23-4

Garage
13-4x23-4

Porch

2-Car Garage with Shop

- Size - 38' x 24'
- Building height - 15'-4"
- Roof pitch - 6/12, 10/12
- Ceiling height - 9'
- Two 9' x 7' overhead doors
- A centrally located shop features built-in cabinetry with window above, plenty of wall space for shop machinery, access to both garages and a covered entry
- Complete list of materials

To order online visit www.projectplans.com

Compact 2-Car Garage

- Size - 20' x 20'
- Building height - 14'
- Roof pitch - 5/12
- Ceiling height - 8'
- 16' x 7' overhead door
- Large garage door makes leaving and entering an easy task
- Complete list of materials

Plan #GM3-059D-6022

Price Code P8

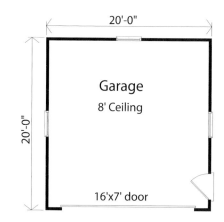

Plan #GM3-063D-6005

Price Code P9

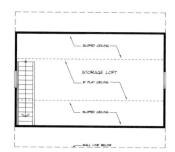

Second Floor

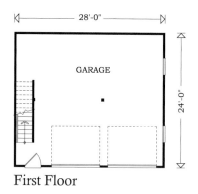

First Floor

2-Car Garage with Loft

- Size - 28' x 24'
- Building height - 22'
- Roof pitch - 12/12
- Ceiling heights -
    First floor - 8'   Second floor - 8'
- Loft ceiling height - 8'
- Two 9' x 7' overhead doors
- Complete list of materials
- Plans are printed on 8 1/2" x 11" pages

Plan #GM3-002D-6032

Price Code P10

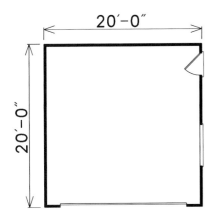

20'-0"

20'-0"

2-Car Economy Garage

- Size - 20' x 20'
- Building height - 11'-10"
- Roof pitch - 4/12
- Ceiling height - 8'
- 16' x 7' overhead door
- Convenient side door
- Complete list of materials
- Step-by-step instructions

Plan #GM3-009D-6018

Price Code P11

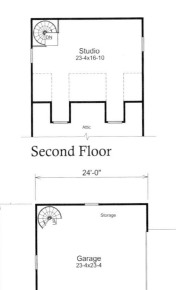

Studio
23-4x16-10

Attic

Second Floor

24'-0"

Storage

Garage
23-4x23-4

30'-0"

Porch

First Floor

2-Car Garage with Studio

- Size - 24' x 30'
- Building height - 21'-4"
- Roof pitch - 4/12, 8/12
- Ceiling heights -
  First floor - 8'   Second floor - 8'
- The oversized garage has a designated rear area for storage and a corner spiral stair to loft above
- Windows provide light to illuminate the second floor loft, perfect for a studio, office or storage
- Complete list of materials

To order online visit www.projectplans.com

2-Car Carport with Storage

Plan #GM3-009D-6015

Price Code P10

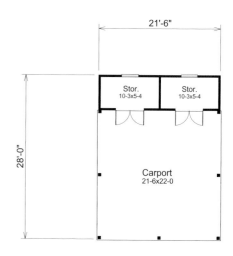

- Size - 21'-6" x 28'-0"
- Building height - 16'-7"
- Roof pitch - 6/12
- Ceiling height - 9'
- Roof dormers with cathedral top louvers, cross-buck doors and other special architectural touches create this eye-catching design
- Located to the rear of the carport are two very functional storage rooms
- Complete list of materials

Plan #GM3-059D-6023

Price Code P8

Compact 2-Car Garage

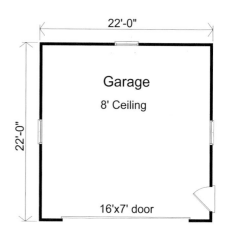

- Size - 22' x 22'
- Building height - 14'
- Roof pitch - 5/12
- Ceiling height - 8'
- 16' x 7' overhead door
- Excellent small garage perfect with many different home styles
- Complete list of materials

To order online visit www.projectplans.com

Plan #GM3-002D-6033

Price Code P10

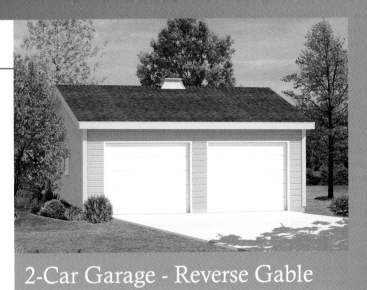

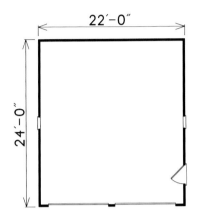

22'-0"

24'-0"

2-Car Garage - Reverse Gable

- Size - 22' x 24'
- Building height - 13'-8"
- Roof pitch - 5/12
- Ceiling height - 8'
- Two 9' x 7' overhead doors
- Complete list of materials
- Step-by-step instructions

Plan #GM3-059D-6024

Price Code P8

22'-0"

22'-0"

Garage

9' Ceiling

16'x7' door

Compact 2-Car Garage

- Size - 22' x 22'
- Building height - 14'
- Roof pitch - 5/12
- Ceiling height - 9'
- 16' x 7' overhead door
- Excellent small garage for many different home styles
- Complete list of materials

2-Car Economy Garage

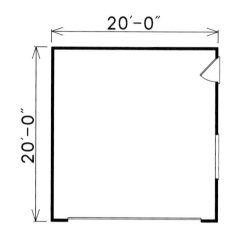

Plan #GM3-002D-6034

Price Code P10

- Size - 20' x 20'
- Building height - 12'
- Roof pitch - 4/12
- Ceiling height - 8'
- 16' x 7' overhead door
- Hip roof design looks good on any lot
- Extended roof over garage door protects from the weather
- Complete list of materials
- Step-by-step instructions

2-Car Garage with Sun Deck

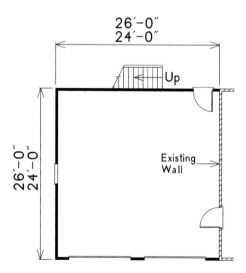

Plan #GM3-064D-6002

Price Code P8

- Sizes -
    24' x 24'
    24' x 26'
    26' x 26'
- Building height - 12'-6"
- Ceiling height - 8'
- Two 9' x 7' overhead doors
- Attached two-car garage with walk-out sun deck
- Complete list of materials
- Step-by-step instructions

Plan #GM3-009D-6014

Price Code P11

Studio/Storage
21-4x14-8

Attic

Second Floor

22'-0"

26'-0"

Entry UP Stor.

2 Car Garage
21-4x21-4

First Floor

2-Car Garage with Studio/Storage

- Size - 22' x 26'
- Building height - 22'
- Roof pitch - 6/12, 10/12
- Ceiling heights -
    First floor - 8'   Second floor - 8'
- Double garage doors, duo lanterns and roof dormers all add a sense of charm to the exterior
- The second floor studio features windows for an abundance of light and a private side entrance
- Complete list of materials

Plan #GM3-059D-6025

Price Code P8

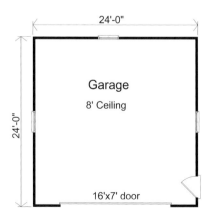

24'-0"

24'-0"

Garage
8' Ceiling

16'x7' door

2-Car Garage

- Size - 24' x 24'
- Building height - 15'
- Roof pitch - 5/12
- Ceiling height - 8'
- 16' x 7' overhead door
- Design complements any home
- Complete list of materials

To order online visit www.projectplans.com

2-Car Garage with Vaulted Loft

- Size - 27' x 27'
- Building height - 21'
- Roof pitch - 8/12
- Ceiling heights -
  First floor - 9'   Second floor - 8'-6"
- Two 9' x 7' overhead doors
- A pull-down, foldable ladder provides access to a convenient vaulted storage loft, well-lit with wall and clerestory windows
- Complete list of materials

Plan #GM3-009D-6012

Price Code P11

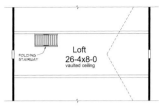

Second Floor

First Floor

2-Car Garage with Storage

- Size - 25' x 26'
- Building height - 21'
- Roof pitch - 10/12
- Ceiling height - 8'
- Two 9' x 7' overhead doors
- Attractive styling with double gabled front facade and decorative window
- Complete list of materials

Plan #GM3-012D-6000

Price Code P10

◄ 25' ►

▲
26'
▼

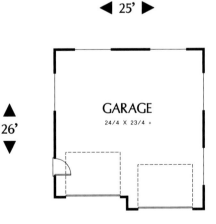

GARAGE
24/4 X 23/4 +

Plan #GM3-002D-6035

Price Code P10

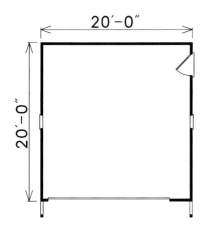

2-Car Economy Garage

- Size - 20' x 20'
- Building height - 12'
- Roof pitch - 4/12
- Ceiling height - 8'
- 16' x 7' garage door
- Practical and functional
- Convenient side door
- Complete list of materials
- Step-by-step instructions

Plan #GM3-059D-6026

Price Code P8

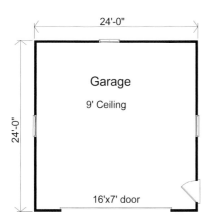

Garage

9' Ceiling

24'-0"

16'x7' door

2-Car Garage

- Size - 24' x 24'
- Building height - 15'
- Roof pitch - 5/12
- Ceiling height - 9'
- 16' x 7' overhead door
- Design complements any home
- Complete list of materials

To order online visit www.projectplans.com

2-Car Garage with Loft

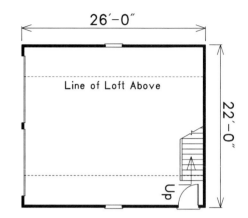

- Size - 22' x 26'
- Building height - 20'-7"
- Roof pitch - 7/12, 12/7
- Ceiling height - 8'
- Loft ceiling height - 7'-4"
- Two 9' x 7' overhead doors
- Complete list of materials
- Step-by-step instructions

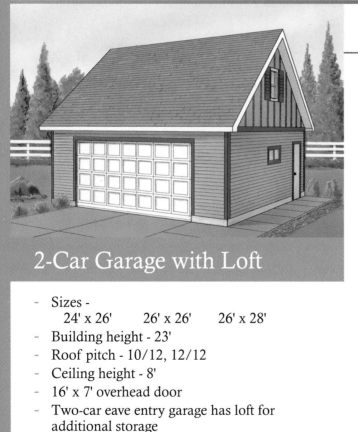

2-Car Garage with Loft

Plan #GM3-064D-6003

Price Code P8

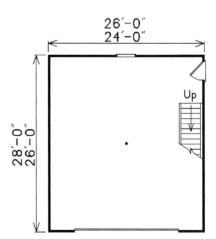

- Sizes -
    24' x 26'   26' x 26'   26' x 28'
- Building height - 23'
- Roof pitch - 10/12, 12/12
- Ceiling height - 8'
- 16' x 7' overhead door
- Two-car eave entry garage has loft for additional storage
- Complete list of materials
- Step-by-step instructions

Plan #GM3-002D-6036

Price Code P10

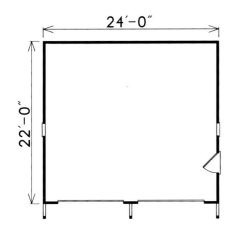

2-Car Garage - Reverse Gable

- Size - 24' x 22'
- Building height - 13'
- Roof pitch - 5/12
- Ceiling height - 8'
- Two 9' x 7' overhead doors
- Roof overhangs garage door to protect from the weather
- Handy side door
- Complete list of materials
- Step-by-step instructions

Plan #GM3-009D-6008

Price Code P11

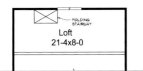

Second Floor

First Floor

2-Car Garage with Loft

- Size - 22'-0" x 25'-4"
- Building height - 20'-6"
- Roof pitch - 3/12, 7/12
- Ceiling heights -
    First floor - 8'   Second floor - 8'
- 18' x 7' overhead door
- The exterior features a roof dormer and service door with decorative brick column and lantern
- Garage has a pull-down stair to the storage loft
- Complete list of materials

To order online visit www.projectplans.com

Plan #GM3-002D-6037

Price Code P11

2-Car Garage with Storage

- Size - 26' x 22'
- Building height - 13'
- Roof pitch - 4/12
- Ceiling height - 8'
- 16' x 7' overhead door
- Provides two separate lockable storage compartments, and one accessible from the outdoors
- Complete list of materials
- Step-by-step instructions

Plan #GM3-059D-6027

Price Code P8

2-Car Garage with Front Gable

- Size - 24' x 24'
- Building height - 14'
- Roof pitch - 5/12
- Ceiling height - 8'
- Two 9' x 7' overhead doors
- Doors add style to this garage design
- Complete list of materials

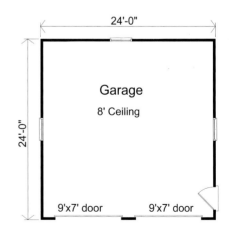

Plan #GM3-002D-6038

Price Code P11

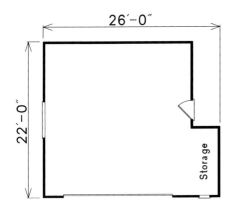

26'-0"

22'-0"

Storage

2-Car Garage with Storage

- Size - 26' x 22'
- Building height - 14'-10"
- Roof pitch - 7/12
- Ceiling height - 8'
- 16' x 7' overhead door
- Attractive salt box style
- Includes additional storage
- Complete list of materials
- Step-by-step instructions

Plan #GM3-009D-6009

Price Code P11

38'-0"

24'-0"

Shop
8-4x13-8

Garage
20-0x23-4

Tractor
Garage
8-4x13-8

Storage
8-4x9-4

Storage
8-4x9-4

Garage with Shop & Storage

- Size - 38' x 24'
- Building height - 21'-6'
- Roof pitch - 8/12
- Ceiling heights -
  Garage - 12'
  Other - 8'
- 16' x 9' overhead door
- Garage features a vaulted ceiling, two storage rooms, rear mower garage and open shop area
- Complete list of materials

To order online visit www.projectplans.com

Plan #GM3-002D-6001

Price Code P11

2-Car Garage with Loft

- Size - 28' x 24'
- Building height - 21'
- Roof pitch - 12/12
- Ceiling height - 8'
- Loft ceiling height - 7'-6"
- Two 9' x 7' overhead doors
- Complete list of materials
- Step-by-step instructions

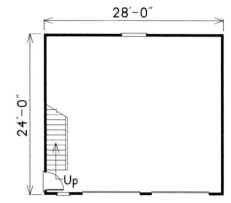

28'-0"

24'-0"

Up

Plan #GM3-059D-6028

Price Code P8

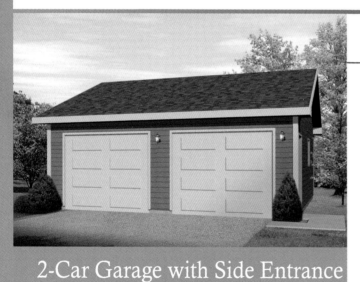

2-Car Garage with Side Entrance

- Size - 24' x 24'
- Building height - 14'
- Roof pitch - 5/12
- Ceiling height - 9'
- Two 9' x 7' overhead doors
- Doors add style to this compact garage design
- Complete list of materials

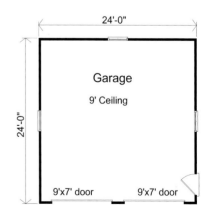

24'-0"

24'-0"

Garage
9' Ceiling

9'x7' door   9'x7' door

Plan #GM3-002D-6039

Price Code P11

28'-0"

24'-0"

Line of Loft Above

Up

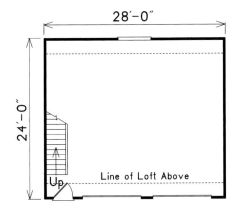

2-Car Garage with Loft

- Size - 28' x 24'
- Building height - 21'
- Roof pitch - 12/12
- Ceiling height - 8'
- Loft ceiling height - 7'-6"
- Two 9' x 7' overhead doors
- Charming dormers add character
- Handy side door accesses stairs to loft
- Complete list of materials

Plan #GM3-009D-6010

Price Code P10

30'-0"

24'-0"

Stor.
10-4x4-4

Stor.
10-4x4-4

Carport
30-0x24-0

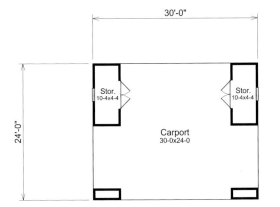

2-Car Carport with Storage

- Size - 30' x 24'
- Building height - 19'-9"
- Roof pitch - 8/12
- Ceiling height - 9'
- An arched window with roof eyebrow and planter box create a certain charm
- Two convenient storage rooms with wide double-entry doors are located at the rear, each brightly lit with a double-hung window
- Complete list of materials

Compact 2-Car Garage

- - Size - 20' x 20'
- - Building height - 14'
- - Roof pitch - 5/12
- - Ceiling height - 8'
- - 16' x 7' overhead door
- - Brick veneer adds elegance to this garage plan
- - Excellent small garage
- - Complete list of materials

Plan #GM3-059D-6029

Price Code P8

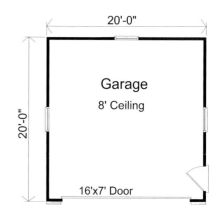

Plan #GM3-108D-6000

Price Code P13

Second Floor

2-Car Garage with Porch

- - Size - 38' x 24'
- - Building height - 24'-8"
- - Roof pitch - 12/12
- - Ceiling heights
    First floor - 8'
    Second Floor - 9'
- - 664 square feet of storage area
- - Slab foundation
- - A sizable covered porch offers the perfect place for outdoor dining and relaxation

First Floor

Plan #GM3-002D-6040

Price Code P10

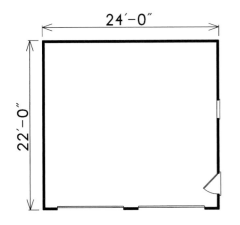

24'-0"

22'-0"

2-Car Garage - Reverse Gable

- Size - 24' x 22'
- Building height - 14'-8"
- Roof pitch - 5/12, 8.5/12
- Ceiling height - 8'
- Two 9' x 7' overhead doors
- Roof overhang above garage doors adds custom look
- Handy side door
- Complete list of materials
- Step-by-step instructions

Plan #GM3-059D-6019

Price Code P9

30'-0"

26'-4"

9' Ceiling

9'x7' Door   9'x7' Door

Stylish 2-Car Garage

- Size - 30'-0" x 26'-4"
- Building height - 17'
- Roof pitch - 6/12, 7/12
- Ceiling height - 9'
- Two 9' x 7' overhead doors
- Plenty of room for vehicles and storage
- Brick veneer adds elegance to this garage plan
- Complete list of materials

To order online visit www.projectplans.com

2-Car Garage with Greenhouse

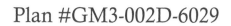

Plan #GM3-002D-6029

Price Code P11

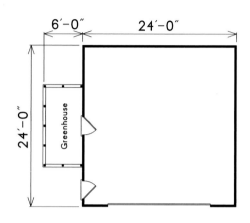

- Size - 30' x 24'
- Building height - 12'-8"
- Roof pitch - 4/12
- Ceiling height - 8'
- 16' x 7' overhead door
- Unique design allows year-round gardening
- Additional space is perfect for storing lawn equipment
- Complete list of materials
- Step-by-step instructions

Plan #GM3-059D-6030

Price Code P8

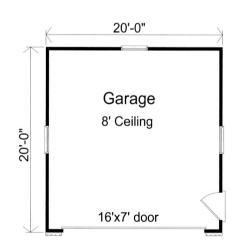

Compact 2-Car Garage

- Size - 20' x 20'
- Building height - 14'
- Roof pitch - 5/12
- Ceiling height - 8'
- 16' x7' overhead door
- Brick veneer adds elegance to this garage plan
- Excellent small garage
- Complete list of materials

Plan #GM3-002D-6002

Price Code P12

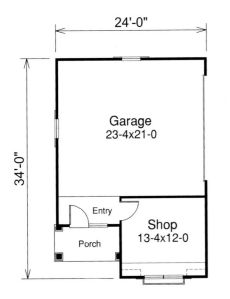

```
         32'-0"
┌─────────────┬──────────────┐
│ Line of Loft │              │
│   Above      │              │
│             │   Garage     │  24'-0"
│ Workshop    │  19-8x23-5   │
│         ┌──┐│              │
│         │Up││              │
└─────────┴──┴──────────────┘
```

2-Car Garage with Workshop

- Size - 32' x 24'
- Building height - 20'-2"
- Roof pitch - 10/12
- Ceiling height - 9'-8"
- Workshop and loft ceiling height - 8'
- 16' x 7' overhead door, 6'-0" x 6'-8" double-door
- Convenient loft above workshop for workspace or storage
- Complete list of materials
- Step-by-step instructions

Plan #GM3-009D-6001

Price Code P12

```
        24'-0"
┌──────────────────┐
│                  │
│     Garage       │
│    23-4x21-0     │  34'-0"
│                  │
│                  │
├────────┬─────────┤
│ Entry  │  Shop    │
│        │13-4x12-0 │
│ Porch  │          │
└────────┴─────────┘
```

2-Car Side Garage with Shop

- Size - 24' x 34'
- Building height - 21'
- Roof pitch - 3/12, 8/12
- Ceiling height - 9'
- 16' x 8' overhead door
- Shop is 13'-4" x 12'-0" with built-in cabinetry
- Porch, roof dormer and shuttered window with planter box provide character
- Complete list of materials

To order online visit www.projectplans.com

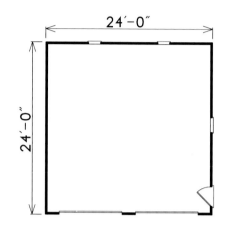

Plan #GM3-002D-6027

Price Code P10

2-Car Garage - Reverse Gable

- Size - 24' x 24'
- Building height - 16'-7"
- Roof pitch - 8/12
- Ceiling height - 8'
- Two 9' x 7' overhead doors
- Easy, functional design
- Complete list of materials
- Step-by-step instructions

Plan #GM3-064D-6004

Price Code P8

2-Car Garage with Loft

- Sizes -
  24' x 26'   26' x 26'   26' x 28'
- Building height - 23'
- Roof pitch - 10/12 or 12/12
- Ceiling height - 8'
- 16' x 7' overhead door
- Two-car garage has loft for additional storage
- Complete list of materials
- Step-by-step instructions

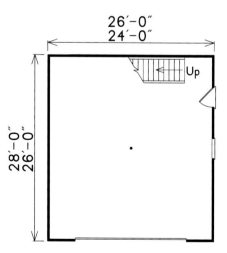

Plan #GM3-002D-6023

Price Code P10

24'-0"

24'-0"

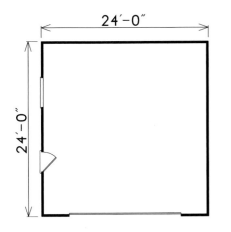

2-Car Garage - Western Style

- Size - 24' x 24'
- Building height - 12'-8"
- Roof pitch - 4/12
- Ceiling height - 8'
- 16' x 7' overhead door
- Appealing style with many homes
- Side-entry door and window are functional extras
- Complete list of materials
- Step-by-step instructions

Plan #GM3-059D-6031

Price Code P8

22'-0"

Garage

9' Ceiling

22'-0"

16'x7' door

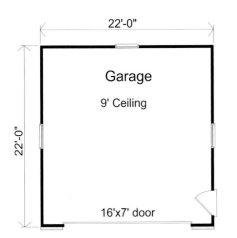

Compact 2-Car Garage

- Size - 22' x 22'
- Building height - 14'
- Roof pitch - 5/12
- Ceiling height - 8'
- 16' x 7' overhead door
- Brick veneer adds elegance to this garage plan
- Excellent small garage for many different home styles
- Complete list of materials

To order online visit www.projectplans.com

2-Car Carport with Storage

Plan #GM3-009D-6002

Price Code P9

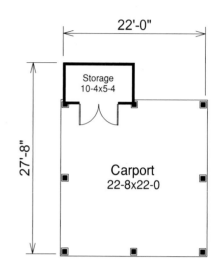

- Size - 22'-0" x 27'-8"
- Building height - 18'
- Roof pitch - 8/12
- Ceiling height - 9'
- Storage shed is 10'-4" x 5'-4" with double-door access
- Stylish details include attic louver, special trim and column moldings
- Complete list of materials

Plan #GM3-059D-6032

Price Code P8

Simple 2-Car Garage

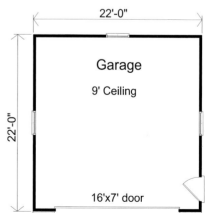

- Size - 22' x 22'
- Building height - 14'
- Roof pitch - 5/12
- Ceiling height - 9'
- 16' x 7' overhead door
- Brick veneer adds elegance to this garage plan
- Complete list of materials

To order online visit www.projectplans.com

Plan #GM3-002D-6021

Price Code P10

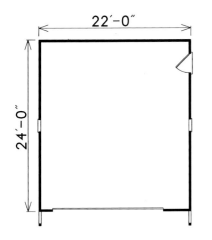

22'-0"

24'-0"

2-Car Garage

- Size - 22' x 24'
- Building height - 12'-2"
- Roof pitch - 4/12
- Ceiling height - 8'
- 16' x 7' overhead door
- Attractive style for any home type
- Appealing side entry
- Complete list of materials
- Step-by-step instructions

Plan #GM3-059D-6033

Price Code P8

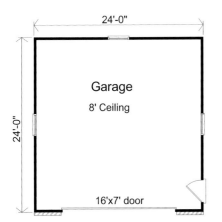

24'-0"

Garage
8' Ceiling

24'-0"

16'x7' door

2-Car Garage

- Size - 24' x 24'
- Building height - 14'
- Roof pitch - 5/12
- Ceiling height - 8'
- 16' x 7' overhead door
- Brick veneer adds elegance to this garage plan
- Complete list of materials

To order online visit www.projectplans.com

Plan #GM3-002D-6013

Price Code P10

2-Car Garage

- Size - 22' x 22'
- Building height - 12'-2"
- Roof pitch - 4/12
- Ceiling height - 8'
- 16' x 7' overhead door
- Useful side entry door
- Perfect for tractor or lawn equipment
- Complete list of materials
- Step-by-step instructions

22'-0"

22'-0"

Plan #GM3-059D-6037

Price Code P9

2-Car Garage with Front Door

- Size - 30' x 26'
- Building height - 17'
- Roof pitch - 6/12, 7/12
- Ceiling height - 9'
- Two 9' x 7' overhead doors
- Front entrance provides easy access
- Complete list of materials

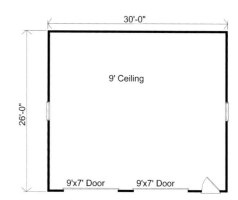

30'-0"

9' Ceiling

26'-0"

9'x7' Door   9'x7' Door

Plan #GM3-002D-6014

Price Code P10

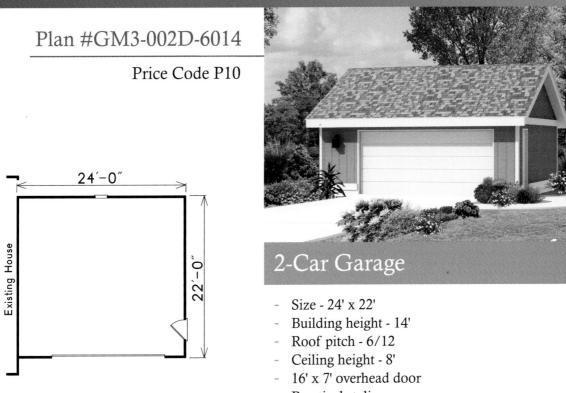

24'-0"

Existing House

22'-0"

2-Car Garage

- Size - 24' x 22'
- Building height - 14'
- Roof pitch - 6/12
- Ceiling height - 8'
- 16' x 7' overhead door
- Practical styling
- Wonderful versatility with this design
- Complete list of materials
- Step-by-step instructions

Plan #GM3-009D-6005

Price Code P12

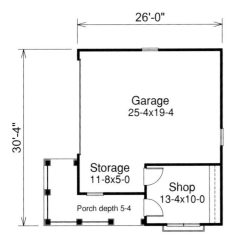

26'-0"

Garage
25-4x19-4

30'-4"

Storage
11-8x5-0

Shop
13-4x10-0

Porch depth 5-4

2-Car Garage with Porch & Shop

- Size - 26'-0" x 30'-4"
- Building height - 19'-4"
- Roof pitch - 8/12, 9/12
- Ceiling height - 8'
- 16' x 7' overhead door
- Shop is 13'-4" x 10'-0" with built-in cabinetry
- Attractive as a front or side garage
- Complete list of materials

To order online visit www.projectplans.com

Plan #GM3-002D-6015

Price Code P11

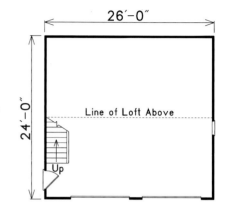

26'-0"
24'-0"
Line of Loft Above
Up

2-Car Garage with Loft

- Size - 26' x 24'
- Building height - 20'
- Roof pitch - 6/12
- Ceiling height - 8'
- Two 9' x 7' overhead doors
- Loft provides extra storage area or workshop space
- Clerestory windows brighten the interior
- Complete list of materials
- Step-by-step instructions

Plan #GM3-059D-6018

Price Code P9

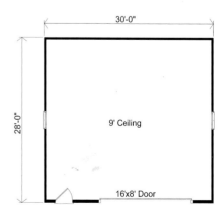

30'-0"
28'-0"
9' Ceiling
16'x8' Door

2-Car Garage with Hip Roof

- Size - 30' x 28'
- Building height - 18'
- Roof pitch - 6/12, 7/12
- Ceiling height - 9'
- 16' x 8' overhead door
- Convenient front door adds style to this garage
- Complete list of materials

Plan #GM3-009D-6006

Price Code P12

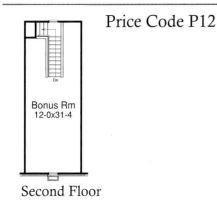

Second Floor

First Floor

Garage with Shop & Bonus Room

- Size - 24' x 32'
- Building height - 22'
- Roof pitch - 10/12
- Ceiling heights -
  First floor - 9'   Second floor - 9'
- 16' x 8' overhead door
- Shop is 9'-9" x 9'-8" with built-in cabinetry
- Attractive as a front or side garage
- Complete list of materials

Plan #GM3-059D-6014

Price Code P10

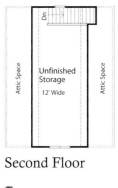

Second Floor

First Floor

2-Car Garage with Western Flair

- Size - 24'-0" x 30'-4"
- Building height - 25'
- Roof pitch - 12/12
- Two 9' x 8' overhead doors
- Ceiling heights -
  First floor - 9'   Second floor - 8'
- Unfinished storage area could easily be converted to a secluded office area
- Brick veneer adds elegance to this garage plan
- Complete list of materials

To order online visit www.projectplans.com

2-Car Garage with Storage

- Size - 24' x 24'
- Building height - 12'-8"
- Roof pitch - 4/12
- Ceiling height - 8'
- 16' x 7' overhead door
- Windows and side door add appeal
- Functional and practical
- Complete list of materials
- Step-by-step instructions

Plan #GM3-002D-6016

Price Code P11

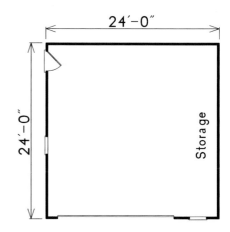

24'-0"

24'-0"

Storage

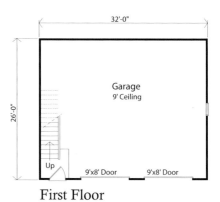

2-Car Garage with Dormers

- Size - 32' x 26'
- Building height - 26'
- Roof pitch - 12/12
- Ceiling heights -
    First floor - 9'
    Second floor - 8'
- Trio of dormers fills unfinished storage with plenty of natural light
- Complete list of materials

Plan #GM3-059D-6013

Price Code P10

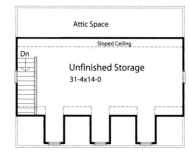

Attic Space

Sloped Ceiling

Dn

Unfinished Storage
31-4x14-0

Second Floor

32'-0"

26'-0"

Garage
9' Ceiling

Up

9'x8' Door   9'x8' Door

First Floor

Plan #GM3-002D-6017

Price Code P11

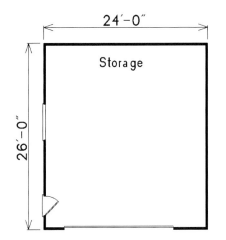

24'-0"

Storage

26'-0"

2-Car Garage with Storage

- Size - 24' x 26'
- Building height - 12'-8"
- Roof pitch - 4/12
- Ceiling height - 8'
- 16' x 7' overhead door
- Plenty of storage space for yard equipment
- Convenient side entry
- Complete list of materials
- Step-by-step instructions

Plan #GM3-059D-6011

Price Code P10

Dn

Attic Space

Unfinished
Storage

12' Wide

Attic Space

Second Floor

24'-0"

Up

30'-0"

Garage

9' Ceiling

9'x8' Door   9'x8' Door

First Floor

2-Car Garage with Storage

- Size - 24' x 30'
- Building height - 25'
- Roof pitch - 12/12
- Two 9' x 8' overhead doors
- Ceiling heights -
    First floor - 9'
    Second floor - 8'
- Attractive cupola adds country charm to the exterior
- Complete list of materials

2-Car Garage - Victorian

- Size - 24' x 24'
- Building height - 16'-7"
- Roof pitch - 8/12
- Ceiling height - 8'
- Two 9' x 7' overhead doors
- Accented with Victorian details
- Functional side entry
- Complete list of materials
- Step-by-step instructions

Plan #GM3-002D-6018

Price Code P10

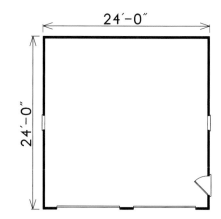

24'-0"

24'-0"

Plan #GM3-059D-6010

Price Code P10

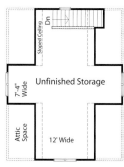

Dn

Sloped Ceiling

7'-4" Wide

Unfinished Storage

Attic Space

12' Wide

Second Floor

28'-0"

30'-0"

Up

Garage
9' Ceiling

4'x6' Porch

9'x8' Door   9'x8' Door

First Floor

2-Car Garage with Gables

- Size - 28' x 30'
- Building height - 25'
- Roof pitch - 12/12
- Two 9' x 8' overhead doors
- Ceiling heights -
    First floor - 9'
    Second floor - 8'
- Attractive cupola and gables are appealing features to this garage
- Complete list of materials

Plan #GM3-009D-6000

Price Code P12

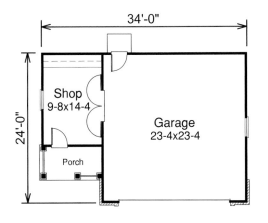

34'-0"

24'-0"

Shop
9-8x14-4

Garage
23-4x23-4

Porch

2-Car Garage with Shop

- Size - 34' x 24'
- Building height - 24'
- Roof pitch - 10/12
- Ceiling height - 9'
- 18' x 8' overhead door
- Shop is 9'-8" x 14'-4" with built-in cabinetry
- Porch, stonework, and shuttered window create charming exterior
- Complete list of materials

Plan #GM3-063D-6010

Price Code P9

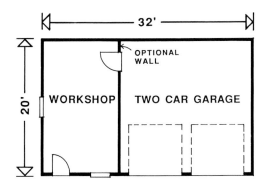

32'

20'

WORKSHOP

OPTIONAL WALL

TWO CAR GARAGE

2-Car Garage with Workshop

- Size - 32' x 20'
- Building height - 13'
- Roof pitch - 5/12
- Ceiling height - 8'
- Two 9' x 7' overhead doors
- Workshop is ideal for storage, gardening or woodworking hobbies
- Outdoor entrance provides quick access
- Complete list of materials

To order online visit www.projectplans.com

Plan #GM3-002D-6019

Price Code P10

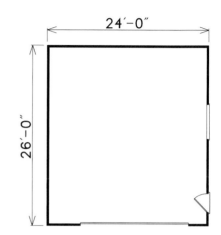

2-Car Garage with High Door

- Size - 24' x 26'
- Building height - 13'-8"
- Roof pitch - 4/12
- Ceiling height - 9'
- 16' x 8' overhead door
- Practical and appealing
- Side window adds light
- Complete list of materials
- Step-by-step instructions

Plan #GM3-059D-6007

Price Code P8

Large 2-Car Garage

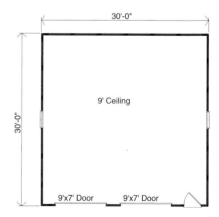

- Size - 30' x 30'
- Building height - 15'
- Roof pitch - 4/12
- Ceiling height - 9'
- Two 9' x 7' overhead doors
- Roomy two-car garage has convenient entry door
- Complete list of materials

Plan #GM3-002D-6009

Price Code P10

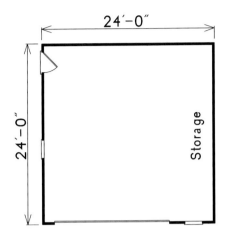

24'-0"

24'-0"

Storage

2-Car Garage with Hip Roof

- Size - 24' x 24'
- Building height - 12'-6"
- Roof pitch - 4/12
- Ceiling height - 8'
- 16' x 7' overhead door
- Side entry provides easy access
- Complete list of materials
- Step-by-step instructions

Plan #GM3-059D-6006

Price Code P8

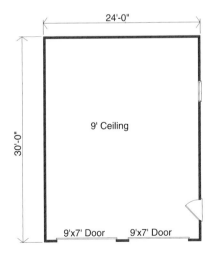

24'-0"

30'-0"

9' Ceiling

9'x7' Door 9'x7' Door

Deep 2-Car Garage

- Size - 24' x 30'
- Building height - 15'
- Roof pitch - 4/12
- Ceiling height - 9'
- Two 9' x 7' overhead doors
- Side entry and window brighten interior
- Complete list of materials

To order online visit www.projectplans.com

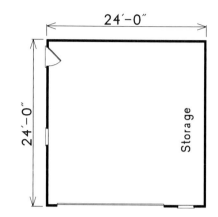

Plan #GM3-002D-6008

Price Code P10

2-Car Garage with Storage

- Size - 24' x 24'
- Building height - 12'-8"
- Roof pitch - 4/12
- Ceiling height - 8'
- 16' x 7' overhead door
- Windows on two sides
- Extra space is perfect for storage
- Complete list of materials
- Step-by-step instructions

Plan #GM3-059D-6005

Price Code P8

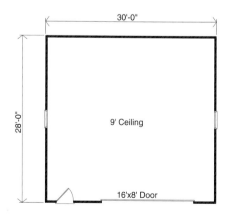

2-Car Garage with Lots of Room

- Size - 30' x 28'
- Building height - 17'
- Roof pitch - 4/12
- Ceiling height - 9'
- 16' x 8' overhead door
- Two side windows brighten interior
- Complete list of materials

To order online visit www.projectplans.com

Plan #GM3-002D-6006

Price Code P10

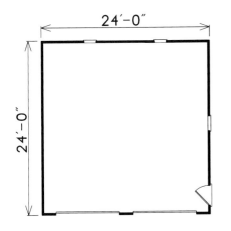

2-Car Garage - Reverse Gable

- Size - 24' x 24'
- Building height - 16'-7"
- Roof pitch - 8/12
- Ceiling height - 8'
- Two 9' x 7' overhead doors
- Oversized, appealing design
- Side door is a handy feature
- Complete list of materials
- Step-by-step instructions

Plan #GM3-059D-6003

Price Code P8

Oversized 2-Car Garage

- Size - 24' x 38'
- Building height - 14'
- Roof pitch - 4/12
- Ceiling height - 9'
- 16' x 7' overhead door
- Convenient side entrance door
- Complete list materials

To order online visit www.projectplans.com

2-Car Garage with Workshop

Plan #GM3-002D-6004

Price Code P12

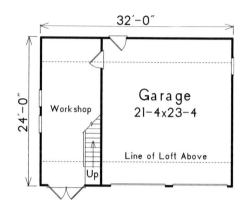

- Size - 32' x 24'
- Building height - 21'
- Roof pitch - 12/12
- Ceiling height - 8'
- Loft ceiling height - 7'-6"
- Two 9' x 7' overhead doors
- Plenty of storage space for workshop or hobby center
- Complete list of materials
- Step-by-step instructions

2-Car Garage with Storage

Plan #GM3-059D-6001

Price Code P9

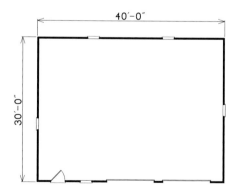

- Size - 40' x 30'
- Building height - 16'-7"
- Roof pitch - 5/12
- Ceiling height - 10'
- Two 10' x 9' overhead doors
- Oversized garage is ideal as a workshop or boat storage
- Complete list of materials

Plan #GM3-002D-6003

Price Code P10

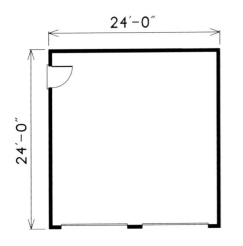

24´-0"

24´-0"

2-Car Garage

- Size - 24' x 24'
- Building height - 12'-6"
- Roof pitch - 4/12
- Ceiling height - 8'
- Two 9' x 7' overhead doors
- Side entry is efficient and well designed
- Complete list of materials
- Step-by-step instructions

Plan #GM3-002D-6041

Price Code P11

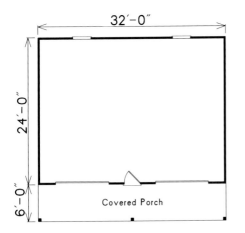

32´-0"

24´-0"

6´-0"

Covered Porch

2 1/2-Car Garage/Roadside Stand

- Size - 32' x 30'
- Building height - 15'-7"
- Roof pitch - 4/12
- Ceiling height - 10'
- Two 9' x 8' overhead doors
- Excellent for displaying, selling and storing fresh produce
- 6' cantilevered front overhang
- Complete list of materials
- Step-by-step instructions

To order online visit www.projectplans.com

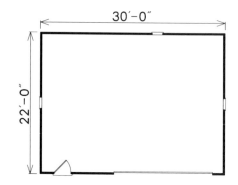

Plan #GM3-002D-6007

Price Code P10

2 1/2-Car Garage

- Size - 30' x 22'
- Building height - 12'-2"
- Roof pitch - 4/12
- Ceiling height - 8'
- 16' x 7' overhead door
- Additional space is perfect for yard equipment storage
- Door allows easy access to and from space
- Complete list of materials
- Step-by-step instructions

30'-0"

22'-0"

Plan #GM3-002D-6024

Price Code P11

2 1/2-Car Garage - Western Style

- Size - 30' x 24'
- Building height - 12'-6"
- Roof pitch - 4/12
- Ceiling height - 8'
- Two 9' x 7' overhead doors
- Plenty of storage space
- Additional space is perfect for workshop
- Complete list of materials
- Step-by-step instructions

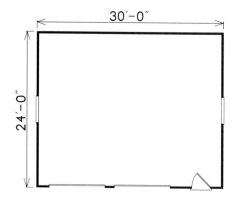

30'-0"

24'-0"

Plan #GM3-009D-6011

Price Code P11

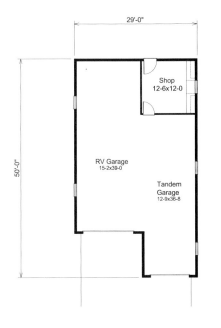

RV & Tandem Garage with Shop

- Size - 29' x 50'
- Building height - 24'-3"
- Roof pitch - 6/12
- Ceiling heights -
    Garage - 9' and 14'
    Shop - 8'
- 9' x 8' and 12' x 12' overhead doors
- The shop includes one wall of cabinetry for a work area and an additional large storage area
- Complete list of materials

Plan #GM3-059D-6012

Price Code P10

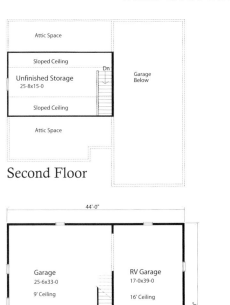

Second Floor

First Floor

RV & 2-Car Garage with Loft

- Size - 44' x 40'
- Building height - 25'
- Roof pitch - 9/12, 10/12
- Ceiling heights -
    First floor - 9'
    Second floor - 8'
- Unfinished storage could easily be converted to an office or workshop
- Complete list of materials

To order online visit www.projectplans.com

RV Garage with Rear Entry

Plan #GM3-009D-7526

Price Code P11

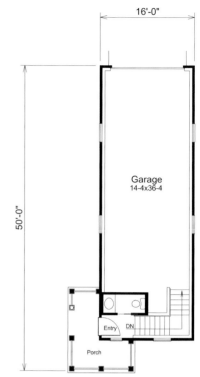

- Size - 16' x 50'
- Building height - 15'
- Roof pitch - 5/12, 8/12
- Ceiling heights -
  Bath, Entry - 8'   Garage - 16'-8"
- 12' x 14' overhead door
- Walk-out basement foundation
- Wrap-around porch leads to an entry foyer with half bath and stairs to the lower level
- Complete list of materials

2-Car & RV Garage with Loft

Plan #GM3-059D-6015

Price Code P10

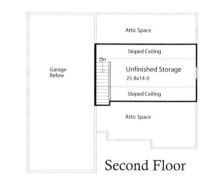

Second Floor

- Size - 44' x 40'
- Building height - 25'
- Roof pitch - 9/12, 10/12
- Ceiling heights -
  First floor - 9', 16'
  Second floor - 8'
- Two 9' x 8', one 12' x 14' overhead doors
- Unfinished storage is ideal for extra camping equipment
- Complete list of materials

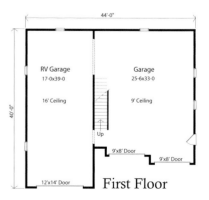

First Floor

Plan #GM3-002D-7500

Price Code P12

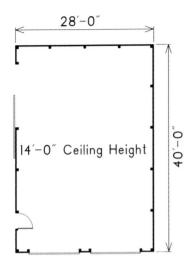

28'-0"

14'-0" Ceiling Height

40'-0"

Pole Building - Shop/Garage

- Size - 28' x 40'
- Building height - 19'-6"
- Roof pitch - 4/12
- Ceiling height - 14'
- Two 10' x 10' overhead doors
- One 12' x 12' sliding door
- Designed for easy maintenance
- Complete list of materials
- Step-by-step instructions

Plan #GM3-059D-6016

Price Code P9

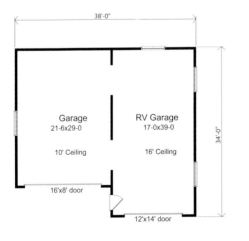

38'-0"

Garage
21-6x29-0

10' Ceiling

RV Garage
17-0x39-0

16' Ceiling

34'-0"

16'x8' door

12'x14' door

1-Car & RV Garage

- Size - 38' x 34'
- Building height - 21'
- Roof pitch - 6/12
- Ceiling heights - 10', 16'
- 16' x 8', 12' x 14' overhead doors
- Excellent garage for large equipment or workshop
- Complete list of materials

To order online visit www.projectplans.com

3-Car Garage with Storage

- Size - 38' x 30'
- Building height - 22'
- Roof pitch - 10/12
- Ceiling height - 9'
- Three 9' x 8' overhead doors
- Attractive styling fits well with most every home
- Complete list of materials

Plan #GM3-012D-6002

Price Code P10

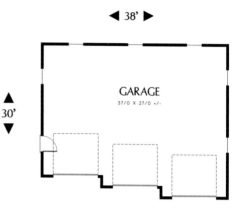

◀ 38' ▶

GARAGE

37/0 X 27/0 +/-

▲
30'
▼

2-Car Garage with RV/Boat Area

- Size - 40' x 40'
- Building height - 21'
- Roof pitch - 6/12
- Ceiling heights - 10', 16'
- 12' x 14', 16' x 8' overhead doors
- Excellent garage for large equipment, RV or boat storage
- Complete list of materials

Plan #GM3-059D-6000

Price Code P9

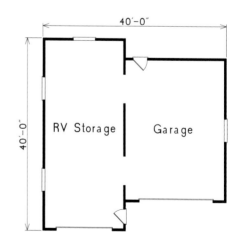

40'-0"

RV Storage | Garage

40'-0"

To order online visit www.projectplans.com

Plan #GM3-002D-6046

Price Code P12

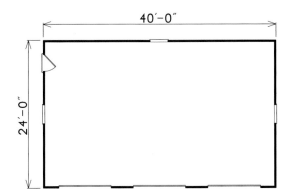

3-Car Garage

- Size - 40' x 24'
- Building height - 15'-6"
- Roof pitch - 6/12
- Ceiling height - 9'
- Three 9' x 7' overhead doors
- Oversized with plenty of room for storage
- Side door for easy access
- Complete list of materials
- Step-by-step instructions

Plan #GM3-059D-6017

Price Code P9

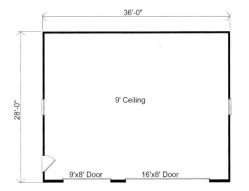

9' Ceiling

9'x8' Door   16'x8' Door

3-Car Garage with Hip Roof

- Size - 36' x 28'
- Building height - 17'
- Roof pitch - 6/12, 7/12
- Ceiling height - 9'
- 9' x 8', 16' x 8' overhead doors
- Charming style complements many homes
- Complete list of materials

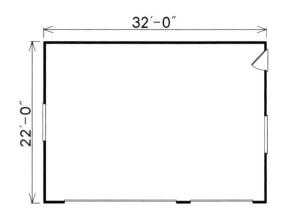

Plan #GM3-002D-6011

Price Code P12

3-Car Garage

- Size - 32' x 22'
- Building height - 12'-2"
- Roof pitch - 4/12
- Ceiling height - 8'
- 9' x 7', 16' x 7' overhead doors
- Side entry for easy access
- Perfect style with many types of homes
- Complete list of materials
- Step-by-step instructions

32'-0"

22'-0"

Plan #GM3-002D-6044

Price Code P12

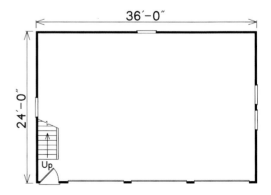

3-Car Garage with Loft

- Size - 36' x 24'
- Building height - 20'-8"
- Roof pitch - 12/12
- Ceiling height - 8'
- Loft ceiling height - 7'-6"
- Three 9' x 7' overhead doors
- Third stall in garage is perfect for boat storage
- Generous loft space for storage or studio
- Complete list of materials
- Step-by-step instructions

36'-0"

24'-0"

Up

To order online visit www.projectplans.com

Plan #GM3-002D-6020

Price Code P12

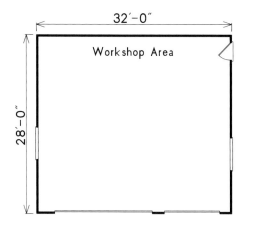

3-Car Garage with Workshop

- Size - 32' x 28'
- Building height - 13'-3"
- Roof pitch - 4/12
- Ceiling height - 8'
- 9' x 7', 16' x 7' overhead doors
- Handy workshop space for hobbies
- Side entry door provides easy access
- Complete list of materials
- Step-by-step instructions

Plan #GM3-002D-6026

Price Code P12

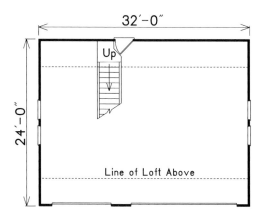

3-Car Garage - Western Style

- Size - 32' x 24'
- Building height - 20'-6"
- Roof pitch - 12/12
- Ceiling height - 8'
- 9' x 7', 16' x 7' overhead doors
- Large side windows draw in light
- Complete list of materials
- Step-by-step instructions

To order online visit www.projectplans.com

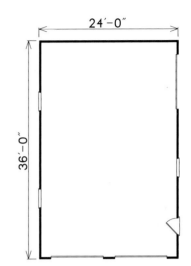

Plan #GM3-002D-6042

Price Code P12

3-Car Garage/Workshop

- Size - 24' x 36'
- Building height - 14'-6"
- Roof pitch - 4/12
- Ceiling height - 10'
- Three 9' x 8' overhead doors
- Oversized for storage
- Ideal size for workshop or maintenance building
- Complete list of materials
- Step-by-step instructions

Plan #GM3-059D-6004

Price Code P9

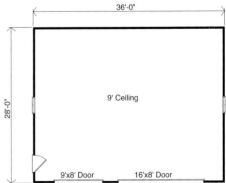

3-Car Garage

- Size - 36' x 28'
- Building height - 17'
- Roof pitch - 4/12
- Ceiling height - 9'
- 9' x 8', 16' x 8' overhead doors
- Versatile style looks good with many different styles of homes
- Complete list of materials

Plan #GM3-002D-6025

Price Code P12

30'-0"

24'-0"

32'-0"

3-Car Garage

- Size - 30' x 24'
- Building height - 13'-8"
- Roof pitch - 5/12
- Ceiling height - 8'
- 9' x 7', 16' x 7' overhead doors
- Highly functional design
- Handy side entry door
- Complete list of materials
- Step-by-step instructions

Plan #GM3-009D-6019

Price Code P12

47'-4"

52'-4"

34'

2 Car Garage
(Below)

RV Garage
(Below)

Balcony Rail

2 Car Garage
23-0x24-8

Entry

Porch

First Floor

2 Car Garage
23-1x21-10

RV Garage
15-2x36-2

Lower Level

4-Car Garage with RV Storage

- Size - 47'-4" x 52'-4"
- Building height - 20'
- Roof pitch - 5/12
- Ceiling heights -
  First floor - 9'   Lower level - 17'-8"
- The upper portion of the garage is perfect for storing two cars in the front while the lower portion easily houses an additional two vehicles and an RV or truck with trailer in the rear
- Complete list of materials

Apartment Garage / Cottage Retreat

Plan #GM3-009D-7516

Price Code P13

- 641 square feet
- Building height - 21'
- Roof pitch - 6/12
- Ceiling heights -
    First floor - 8'
    Second floor - 8'
- 9' x 7' overhead door
- Charming exterior enjoys a wrap-around porch and a large feature window with arch and planter box
- Complete list of materials

Second Floor

Bedroom
15-10x11-8

Plant shelf below

DN

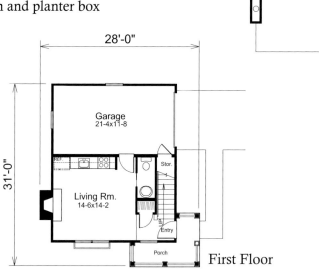

28'-0"

31'-0"

Garage
21-4x11-8

REF.

Stor.

Living Rm.
14-6x14-2

UP

Entry

Porch

First Floor

Plan #GM3-009D-7514

Price Code P13

17'-0"

Patio

Office/Workshop
16-4x11-8

ENTRY

34'-0"

Garage
12-4x21-4

UP

ENTRY

First Floor
286 sq. ft.

REF

DW

Kit/Liv. Rm.
16-4x11-8

DN

W
WH

Second Floor
370 sq. ft.

Studio Apartment Garage with Office

- 656 square feet
- Building height - 23'
- Roof pitch - 7/12
- Ceiling heights -
    First floor - 8'
    Second floor - 8'
- 9' x 7' overhead door
- Located behind the garage is the perfect room for an office or workshop and has glass sliding doors to a rear patio
- A well-equipped kitchenette, full bath and a closet/mechanical room are the featured spaces of the efficient studio apartment
- Complete list of materials

To order online visit www.projectplans.com

1-Car Garage with Studio Apartment

Plan #GM3-009D-7531

Price Code P13

- 314 square feet
- Building height - 22'-5"
- Roof pitch - 4/12, 8.5/12
- Ceiling heights -
    First floor - 8'
    Second floor - 8
- 9' x 7' overhead door
- Slab foundation
- The first floor consists of a 1-car garage, laundry room, mechanical closet and an entry with a door to the outdoors and stairs to the second floor
- The second floor features a studio apartment complete with a well-equipped kitchenette alcove, closet and private bath
- Complete list of materials

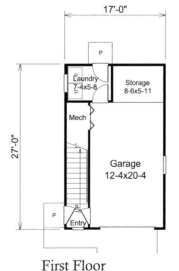

First Floor
105 sq. ft.

Second Floor
237 sq. ft.

Plan #GM3-009D-7533

Price Code P13

First Floor

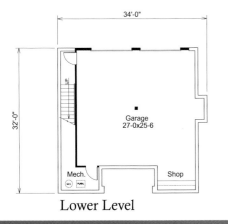

Lower Level

2-Car Garage, Game Room & Bar

- 960 square feet
- Building height - 17'
- Roof pitch - 5/12, 8/12
- Ceiling heights -
  First floor - 8'   Second floor - 8'
- Two 9' x 7' overhead doors
- Walk-out basement foundation
- The first floor game room/sports bar features a movie theater with 10' wide screen, fireplace, kitchen/wet bar, bath, closets and a front entry porch
- The lower level consists of a rear entry garage, shop area and storage room
- Complete list of materials

Garage with Shop & Safety Shelter

Plan #GM3-009D-7523

Price Code P11

- Building height - 17'-6"
- Roof pitch - 8/12
- Ceiling heights -
    First floor - 8'
    Lower level - 7'-10"
- 18' x 7' overhead door
- Slab foundation
- Multiple gables, box window and stonework add up to an attractive facade
- Large multi-purpose room is perfect for a shop, studio or office and includes cabinetry, a half bath, access to garage and stairs to the lower level safety shelter
- Complete list of materials

First Floor

Lower Level

To order online visit www.projectplans.com

Plan #GM3-002D-7528

Price Code P13

Second Floor

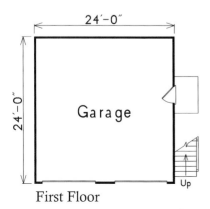

First Floor

2-Car Garage Apartment

- 576 square feet
- Building height - 21'-5"
- Roof pitch - 4/12
- Ceiling heights -
   First floor - 8'
   Second floor - 8'
- Two 9' x 7' overhead doors
- 1 bedroom, 1 bath
- Loft has roomy kitchen and dining area
- Private side exterior entrance
- Style complements many types of homes
- Complete list of materials
- Step-by-step instructions

To order online visit www.projectplans.com

Home Sports Bar with Movie Theater

Plan #GM3-009D-7522

Price Code P13

- 1,170 square feet
- Building height - 25'-6"
- Roof pitch - 5/12, 8/12
- Ceiling heights -
    First floor - 8'
    Second floor - 8'
- Two 10' x 7' overhead doors
- Slab foundation
- The first floor has a 2-car garage with shop, office, storage and mechanical closets
- The second floor features a movie theater with 10' screen, fireplace, wet bar, bath and three closets
- Complete list of materials

Second Floor
960 sq. ft.

First Floor
210 sq. ft.

Plan #GM3-009D-7515

Price Code P13

Apartment Garage Plus RV Storage

- 713 square feet
- Building height - 25'
- Roof pitch - 3.5/12, 6.5/12
- Ceiling heights -
    First floor - 9'
    Second floor - 8'
    RV garage - 13'-4"
- 18' x 8', 12' x 12' overhead doors
- Complete list of materials

Second Floor

Bedroom
15-10x12-0

Hall

Attic

Attic

38'-8"

42'-4"

First Floor

Dine

Kitchen
8-1x8-6

Living Rm.
13-3x12-0

Entry

RV Garage
16-2x31-2

2-Car Garage
21-4x23-8

2-Car Garage Apartment

- 438 square feet
- Building height - 21'-3"
- Roof pitch - 6/12, 12/6
- Ceiling heights -
    First floor - 8'
    Second floor - 7'-9"
- Two 9' x 7' overhead doors
- Comfortable colonial styling
- Simple yet spacious studio design
- Large windows warm interior
- Complete list of materials
- Step-by-step instructions

Plan #GM3-002D-7527

Price Code P13

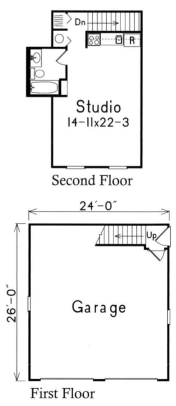

Studio
14-11x22-3

Second Floor

24'-0"

26'-0"

Up

Garage

First Floor

Plan #GM3-059D-7510

Price Code P12

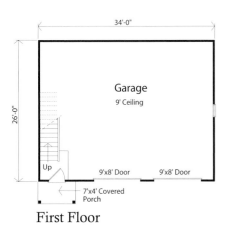

Attic Space

Dn

P R L

Sitting
10-9x14-0

Kit.

Sleeping
9-2x8-8

Second Floor

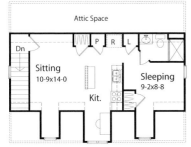

34'-0"

26'-0"

Garage
9' Ceiling

Up

9'x8' Door   9'x8' Door

7'x4' Covered
Porch

First Floor

2-Car Garage Apartment

- 568 square feet
- Building height - 26'
- Roof pitch - 12/12
- Ceiling heights -
   First floor - 9'
   Second floor - 8'
- 1 bedroom/sleeping area, 1 bath
- Beautiful dormers brighten interior
- Complete list of materials

Cozy 2-Car Garage Apartment

- 615 square feet
- Building height - 25'-4"
- Roof pitch - 8/12, 10/12
- Ceiling heights -
    First floor - 8'
    Second floor - 8'
- 16' x 7' overhead door
- Living room enjoys a fireplace with shelving and is open to the kitchen with an eating area
- Lots of closet space
- Complete list of materials

Plan #GM3-009D-7513

Price Code P13

Second Floor

First Floor

Plan #GM3-009D-7510

Price Code P13

2-Car Apartment Garage

- 588 square feet
- Building height - 16'-6"
- Roof pitch - 7/12, 8/12
- Ceiling height - 8'
- 18' x 7' overhead door
- 1 bedroom, 1 bath
- Living room features a functional entry, bayed dining area, corner fireplace and opens to kitchen with breakfast bar
- Complete list of materials

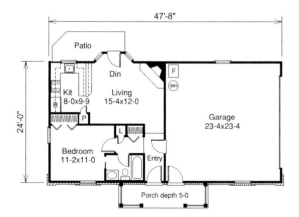

47'-8"

24'-0"

Patio

Din

Kit
8-0x9-9

Living
15-4x12-0

F

WH

P

R

Garage
23-4x23-4

Bedroom
11-2x11-0

L

Entry

Porch depth 5-0

To order online visit www.projectplans.com

2-Car Garage Apartment - Cape Cod

Plan #GM3-002D-7526

Price Code P13

- 566 square feet
- Building height - 22'
- Roof pitch - 4.5/12, 12/12
- Ceiling heights -
    First floor - 8'
    Second floor - 7'-7"
- Two 9' x 7' overhead doors
- Charming dormers add appeal to this design
- Comfortable open living area
- Complete list of materials
- Step-by-step instructions

Second Floor

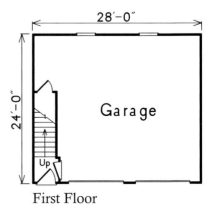

First Floor

Plan #GM3-009D-7507

Price Code P12

2-Car Garage with Office

- 434 square feet
- Building height - 18'
- Roof pitch - 8/12
- Ceiling height - 8'
- 16' x 7' overhead door
- Office features an entry closet, storage closet, toilet room and stairs to basement shelter
- Complete list of materials

To order online visit www.projectplans.com

RV & 2-Car Garage with Shop

Plan #GM3-009D-7506

Price Code P12

- Size - 46' x 38'
- Building height - 21'-4"
- Roof pitch - 7/12, 8/12
- Ceiling heights - 9', 16'
- 16' x 7', 12' x 14' overhead doors
- Shop is 11'-0" x 12'-2" and includes built-in cabinets and half bath
- Pleasing exterior disguises RV side-garage with a one-story look
- Complete list of materials

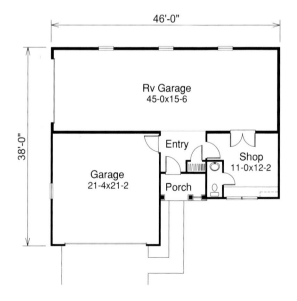

Plan #GM3-002D-7525

Price Code P13

Kit 9-0x9-4

Studio
23-4x14-0

Dn

Second Floor

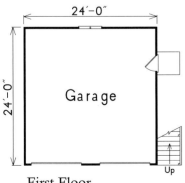

24'-0"

24'-0"

Garage

Up

First Floor

2-Car Garage Apartment - Studio

- 576 square feet
- Building height - 21'-6"
- Roof pitch - 4/12
- Ceiling heights -
    First floor - 8'
    Second floor - 8'
- Two 9' x 7' overhead doors
- Contemporary style with private outdoor entrance
- Complete list of materials
- Step-by-step instructions

To order online visit www.projectplans.com

2-Car Garage Apartment

- 652 square feet
- Building height - 23'
- Roof pitch - 3.5/12, 11/12
- Ceiling heights -
    First floor - 8'
    Second floor - 8'
- Two 9' x 7' overhead doors
- 1 bedroom, 1 bath
- Cozy U-shaped kitchen is convenient to the dining and living rooms
- Complete list of materials

Plan #GM3-063D-7503

Price Code P11

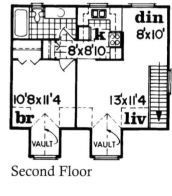

Second Floor

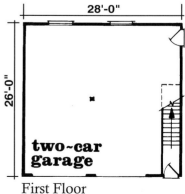

First Floor

Plan #GM3-002D-7524

Price Code P13

Studio
17-4x14-7

Kitchen

Dining

Dn

R

L

Second Floor

```
|←——— 28'-0" ———→|
```

Garage

24'-0"

F

Up

First Floor

2-Car Garage - Gambrel Roof

- 604 square feet
- Building height - 21'-4"
- Roof pitch - 4/12, 12/4.75
- Ceiling heights -
    First floor - 8'
    Second floor - 8'
- Two 9' x 7' overhead doors
- Charming Dutch-Colonial style
- Spacious studio provides extra storage space
- Complete list of materials
- Step-by-step instructions

To order online visit www.projectplans.com

2-Car Garage Apartment

- 628 square feet
- Building height - 26'-6"
- Roof pitch - 8/12, 9/12
- Ceiling heights -
  First floor - 9'
  Second floor - 8'
- 16' x 7' overhead door
- 1 bedroom, 1 bath
- Cozy living room offers vaulted ceiling, fireplace and a pass-through kitchen
- Complete list of materials

Plan #GM3-009D-7502

Price Code P13

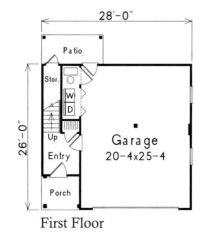

First Floor

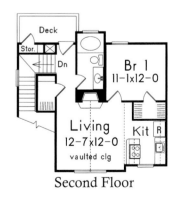

Second Floor

Plan #GM3-012D-7501

Price Code P13

Garage Apartment

- 633 square feet
- Building height - 24'
- Roof pitch - 9/12
- Ceiling heights -
  First floor - 8'
  Second floor - 8'
- 1 bedroom, 1 bath
- Two 8' x 7' overhead doors
- Lots of storage throughout including built-in shelves and a desk in the living area
- Complete list of materials

Second Floor

◄ 28' ►

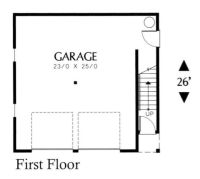

First Floor

2-Car Garage - Western Style

- 784 square feet
- Building height - 24'-6"
- Roof pitch - 6/12
- Ceiling heights -
    First floor - 8'
    Second floor - 8'
- Two 9' x 7' overhead doors
- 1 bedroom, 1 bath
- Open living area is spacious and functional
- Space for utilities off the kitchen
- Complete list of materials
- Step-by-step instructions

Plan #GM3-002D-7519

Price Code P12

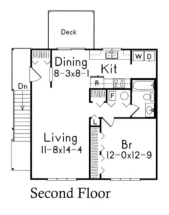

Second Floor

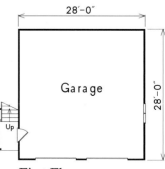

First Floor

Plan #GM3-059D-7508

Price Code P12

Second Floor

First Floor

2-Car Garage Apartment

- 1,240 square feet
- Building height - 27'
- Roof pitch - 6/12, 9/12, 12/12
- Ceiling heights -
    First floor - 9'
    Second floor - 8'
- 2 bedrooms, 1 bath
- Kitchen/breakfast area combine for added spaciousness
- Sloped ceiling adds appeal in the sitting area
- Complete list of materials

2-Car Garage Apartment

- 588 square feet
- Building height - 23'
- Roof pitch - 4/12, 12/12
- Ceiling heights -
    First floor - 8'
    Second floor - 8'
- Two 9' x 7' overhead doors
- 1 bedroom, 1 bath
- Charming dormers add character to exterior
- Convenient laundry space in kitchen
- Complete list of materials

Plan #GM3-063D-7502

Price Code P11

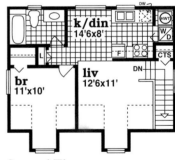

Second Floor

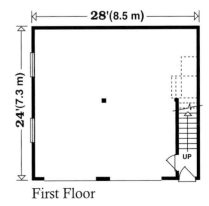

First Floor

Plan #GM3-002D-7510

Price Code P13

Second Floor

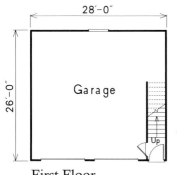

First Floor

2-Car Garage with Interior Entrance

- 746 square feet
- Building height - 22'
- Roof pitch - 4/12
- Ceiling heights -
    First floor - 8'
    Second floor - 8'
- Two 9' x 7' overhead doors
- 1 bedroom, 1 bath
- Complete list of materials
- Step-by-step instructions

3-Car Garage Apartment

- 676 square feet
- Building height - 22'
- Roof pitch - 12/12
- Ceiling heights -
    First floor - 8'
    Second floor - 8'
- 9' x 7' and 16' x 7' overhead doors
- 1 bedroom, 1 bath
- L-shaped kitchen joins the living area to create an open feeling
- Complete list of materials

Plan #GM3-063D-7504

Price Code P11

Second Floor

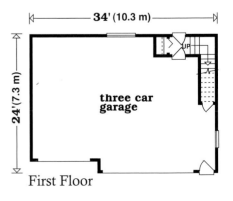

First Floor

Plan #GM3-009D-7500

Price Code P13

Second Floor

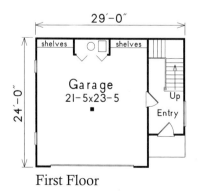

First Floor

2-Car Garage Apartment

- 654 square feet
- Building height - 24'
- Roof pitch - 7/12
- Ceiling heights -
    First floor - 8'
    Second floor - 8'
- 16' x 7' overhead door
- 1 bedroom, 1 bath
- Vaulted living room is open to a pass-through kitchen and breakfast bar with an overhead plant shelf and sliding glass doors to an outdoor balcony
- Complete list of materials

To order online visit www.projectplans.com

3-Car Carport with Apartment

- 672 square feet
- Building height - 22' with 8' carport height
- Roof pitch - 4/12
- 1 bedroom, 1 bath
- Apartment can double as a vacation getaway
- Complete list of materials
- Step-by-step instructions

Plan #GM3-002D-7516

Price Code P13

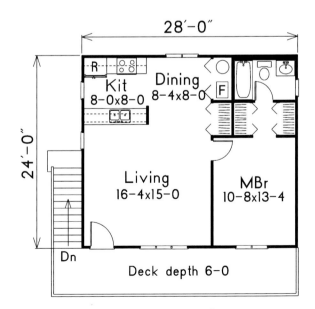

To order your project plan use the form on page 160 or call toll-free 1-800-373-2646

Plan #GM3-059D-7509

Price Code P12

Second Floor

Br 1
11-8x12-0

Kit./Brk
21-0x10-4

Br 2
12-1x11-7

Family
20-0x15-7

40'-0"
30'-0"

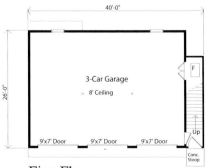

First Floor

3-Car Garage
8' Ceiling

40'-0"
26'-0"

9'x7' Door   9'x7' Door   9'x7' Door

Conc. Stoop

Up

F

3-Car Garage Apartment

- 1,032 square feet
- Building height - 24'
- Roof pitch - 5/12, 10/12
- Ceiling heights -
    First floor - 8'
    Second floor - 8'
- 2 bedrooms, 1 bath
- Three 9' x 7' overhead doors
- Spacious family room flows into kitchen/breakfast area
- Two sunny bedrooms share a bath
- Complete list of materials

To order online visit www.projectplans.com

3-Car Garage Apartment

- 1,040 square feet
- Building height - 23'
- Roof pitch - 5/12
- Ceiling heights -
    First floor - 8'
    Second floor - 8'
- Three 9' x 7' overhead doors
- 2 bedrooms, 1 bath
- Large rooms offer comfortable living with second floor laundry, ample cabinets and sliding doors to deck
- Complete list of materials

Plan #GM3-002D-7529

Price Code P13

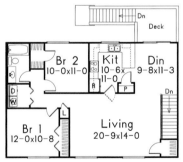

Second Floor

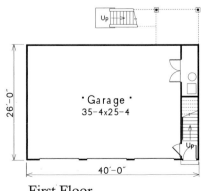

First Floor

Plan #GM3-059D-7507

Price Code P12

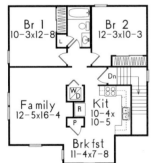

Second Floor

Br 1
10-3x12-8

Br 2
12-3x10-3

Family
12-5x16-4

Kit
10-4x
10-5

W/D
R
P

Dn

Brk fst
11-4x7-8

First Floor

31'-4"

32'-0"

Storage
7-4x12-4

Garage
31-0x22-11

Up

3-Car Garage with Storage

- 973 square feet
- Building height - 24'-8"
- Roof pitch - 6/12
- Ceiling heights -
    First floor - 8'
    Second floor - 8'
- 2 bedrooms, 1 bath
- 9' x 7', 16' x 7' overhead doors
- Sunny breakfast room is positioned between the kitchen and the family room for convenience
- Complete list of materials

To order online visit www.projectplans.com

3-Car Garage - Cape Cod

- 813 square feet
- Building height - 22'
- Roof pitch - 4.25/12, 12/12
- Ceiling heights -
    First floor - 8'
    Second floor - 8'
- Three 9' x 7' overhead doors
- Studio, 1 bath
- Spacious studio apartment has a kitchen and bath
- Perfect for recreation, in-law suite or home office
- Complete list of materials

Plan #GM3-002D-7530

Price Code P13

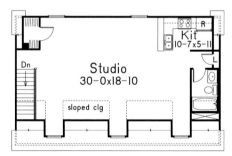

Second Floor

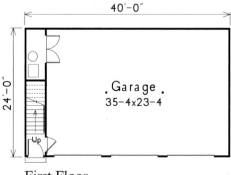

First Floor

Plan #GM3-059D-7506

Price Code P12

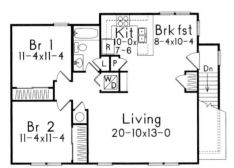

Second Floor

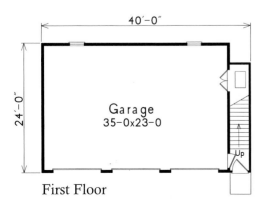

First Floor

3-Car Garage Apartment

- 974 square feet
- Building height - 23'-2"
- Roof pitch - 5/12
- Ceiling heights -
    First floor - 8'
    Second floor - 8'
- 2 bedrooms, 1 bath
- Three 9' x 7' overhead doors
- Efficiently designed kitchen and breakfast room combine with living area for spaciousness
- Complete list of materials

To order online visit www.projectplans.com

3-Car Garage with Country Flair

- 929 square feet
- Building height - 27'
- Roof pitch - 6.5/12, 10/12
- Ceiling heights -
  First floor - 9'
  Second floor - 8'
- 9' x 8', 16' x 8' overhead doors
- 2 bedrooms, 1 bath, 3-car side entry garage
- Spacious living room with dining area has access to 8' x 12' deck
- Complete list of materials

Plan #GM3-009D-7504

Price Code P13

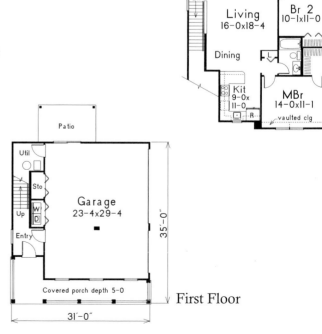

Second Floor

Deck

Living 16-0x18-4

Br 2 10-1x11-0

Dining

Kit 9-0x 11-0

MBr 14-0x11-1
vaulted clg

First Floor

Patio

Util

Sto

Up

W D

Entry

Garage 23-4x29-4

35'-0"

Covered porch depth 5-0

31'-0"

Plan #GM3-059D-7504

Price Code P12

Second Floor

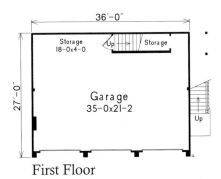

First Floor

3-Car Garage Apartment

- 949 square feet
- Building height - 24'-10"
- Roof pitch - 6/12
- Ceiling heights -
  First floor - 9'
  Second floor - 8'
- 1 bedroom, 1 bath
- Three 9' x 7' overhead doors
- Sitting area includes an attractive window seat which becomes the focal point
- Complete list of materials

3-Car Garage with Rear Apartment

- 1,005 square feet
- Building height - 25'
- Roof pitch - 3.5/12, 6/12, 8/12
- Ceiling heights -
    First floor - 9'
    Second floor - 8'
- Three 9' x 8' overhead doors
- 2 bedrooms, 1 1/2 baths, 3-car garage
- Two-story apartment is disguised with one-story facade featuring triple garage doors and roof dormer
- Complete list of materials

Plan #GM3-009D-7509

Price Code P13

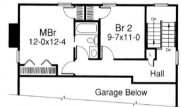

Second Floor

First Floor

Plan #GM3-012D-7500

Price Code P11

Second Floor

First Floor

3-Car Garage with Bonus Room

- 686 square feet on second floor
- Building height - 25'-6"
- Roof pitch - 10/12
- Ceiling heights -
  First floor - 12'
  Second floor - 8'
- Bath on first floor and convenient bonus room on second floor
- Three 9' x 10' overhead doors
- Vaulted bonus room would make an ideal home office or hobby area
- Complete list of materials

To order online visit www.projectplans.com

3-Car Garage with Bonus Rooms

Plan #GM3-009D-7517

Price Code P12

- 967 square feet
- Building size - 32'-8" x 34'-4"
- Building height - 25'
- Roof pitch - 10/12
- Ceiling heights -
    First floor - 9'
    Second floor - 8'
- Three 9' x 8' overhead doors
- Slab foundation
- Hall from garage provides access to room ideal for office or workshop, a half bath, stair to second floor bonus room and door to exterior
- Complete list of materials

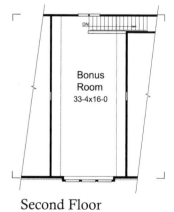

Second Floor
564 sq. ft.

First Floor
403 sq. ft.

Plan #GM3-009D-7521

Price Code P13

Second Floor
439 sq. ft.

First Floor
587 sq. ft.

4-Car Apartment Garage with Style

- 1,026 square feet
- Building height - 25'
- Roof pitch - 8/12
- Ceiling heights -
  First floor - 9'
  Second floor - 8'
- Two 16' x 7' overhead doors
- 1 bedroom, 1 1/2 baths, 4-car garage
- Slab foundation
- A one-story look, clerestory roof dormer and nice symmetry all help to create this handsome exterior
- Complete list of materials

To order online visit www.projectplans.com

Construction Blueprints...

FULLY DETAILED BLUEPRINTS AVAILABLE
for all projects featured in this book.

Blueprint Plans include the following:

- A complete list of materials
- Fully dimensioned details

- Framing plans
- Framing elevations

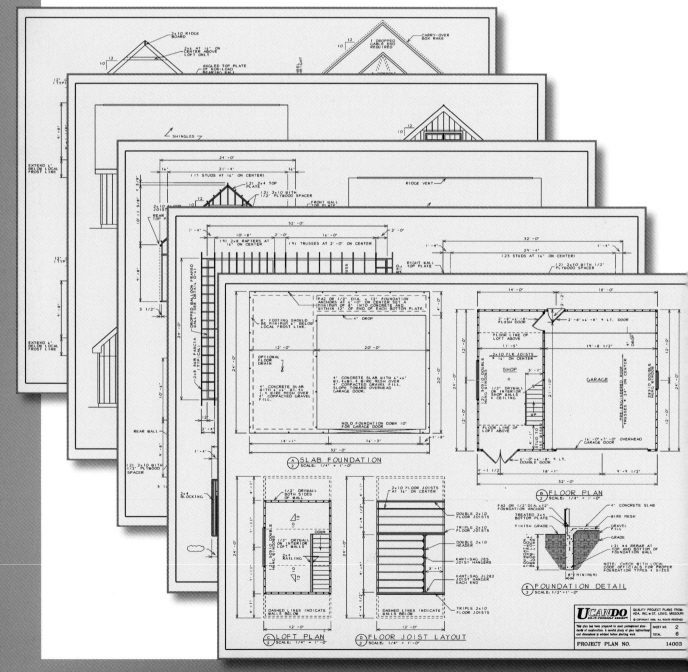

Project Plan Index

How To Order

For fastest service, Call Toll-Free
1-800-DREAM HOME
(1-800-373-2646) day or night

FOUR Easy Ways To Order

1. CALL toll-free 1-800-373-2646 for credit card orders. MasterCard, Visa, Discover and American Express are accepted.

2. FAX your order to 1-314-770-2226.

3. MAIL the Order Form to:

   HDA, Inc.
   944 Anglum Road
   St. Louis, MO 63042
   Attn: Customer Service Dept.

4. ONLINE visit www.projectplans.com

QUESTIONS?
Call Our Customer Service Number
314-770-2228

Order Form

Please send me -

PLAN NUMBER GM3- _____

PRICE CODE _____ (see Plan Page)

Reproducible Masters (call for availability)	$ _____
CAD Package (call for availability)	$ _____
PDF File	$ _____
One-Set of Plans	$ _____
Additional Plan Sets*** (see chart at right)	
_____ (Qty) at $ _____ each	$ _____
SUBTOTAL	$ _____
SALES TAX (MO residents add 7%)	$ _____
☐ Shipping / Handling (see chart at right)	$ _____

(each additional set add $2.00 to shipping charges)

TOTAL ENCLOSED (US funds only) $ _____

☐ Enclosed is my check or money order payable to HDA, Inc. (Sorry, no COD's)

I hereby authorize HDA, Inc. to charge this purchase to my credit card account (check one):

☐ MasterCard ☐ VISA ☐ DISCOVER ☐ AMERICAN EXPRESS Cards

Credit Card number _____

Expiration date _____

Signature _____

Name _____
(Please print or type)

Street Address _____
(Please **do not** use PO Box)

City _____

State _____ Zip _____

Daytime phone number (_____) - _____

E-mail _____

Thank you for your order!

Important Information to Know Before You Order

♦ **Exchange Policies -** Since blueprints are printed in response to your order, we cannot honor requests for refunds. However, if for some reson you find that the plan you have purchased does not meet your requirements, you may exchange that plan for another plan in our collection within 90 days of purchase. At the time of the exchange, you will be charged a processing fee of 25% of your original plan package price, plus the difference in price between the plan packages (if applicable) and the cost to ship the new plans to you.

   Please note: Reproducible drawings can only be exchanged if the package is unopened and a 25% restocking fee will be charged.

♦ **Building Codes & Requirements -** At the time the construction drawings were prepared, every effort was made to ensure that these plans and specifications met nationally recognized codes. Our plans conform to most national building codes. Because building codes vary from area to area, some drawing modifications and/or the assistance of a professional designer or architect may be necessary to comply with your local codes or to accommodate specific building site conditions. We advise you to consult with your local building official for information regarding codes governing your area.

♦ **PDF File Format -** A complete set of construction drawings in an electronic format that allows you to modify and reproduce the plans to fit your needs. Since these are electronic files, we can send them to you within 24 hours (Mon-Fri, 8-5 CST) via email and save you shipping costs. They also offer printing flexibility by allowing you to print the size and number of sets you need. Note: These are not CAD files and cannot be altered electronically.

♦ **CAD Packages -** Many of our plans are available in CAD. For availability, please call our Customer Service Number at 1-800-373-2646.

Blueprint Price Schedule

Price Code	1-Set	Additional Sets	Reproducible Masters/ PDF Files
P6	$40.00	$15.00	$90.00
P7	$60.00	$15.00	$110.00
P8	$125.00	$20.00	$175.00
P9	$175.00	$25.00	$225.00
P10	$200.00	$25.00	$250.00
P11	$225.00	$30.00	$275.00
P12	$250.00	$30.00	$300.00
P13	$310.00	$45.00	$610.00

Plan prices subject to change without notice.
Please note that plans are not refundable.

Shipping & Handling Charges

EACH ADDITIONAL SET ADD $2.00 TO SHIPPING CHARGES

U.S. SHIPPING - (AK and HI express only)

Regular (allow 7-10 business days)	$5.95
Priority (allow 3-5 business days)	$15.00
Express* (allow 1-2 business days)	$25.00

CANADA SHIPPING

Standard (allow 8-12 business days)	$15.00
Express* (allow 3-5 business days)	$40.00

OVERSEAS SHIPPING/INTERNATIONAL
Call, fax, or e-mail (plans@hdainc.com) for shipping costs.

* For express delivery please call us by 11:00 a.m. Monday-Friday CST

** Orders may be subject to custom's fees and or duties/taxes.

*** An additional set cannot be ordered without the purchase of an initial set or reproducible masters.

NOTE: Shipping and handling does not apply on PDF files. Orders will be emailed within 24 hours (Mon-Fri., 8-5 CST) of purchase.